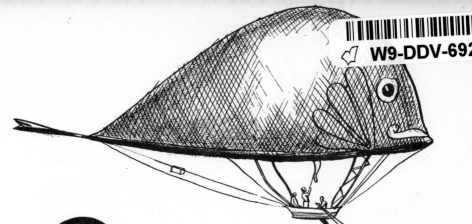

Ripley's Believe It or Not!

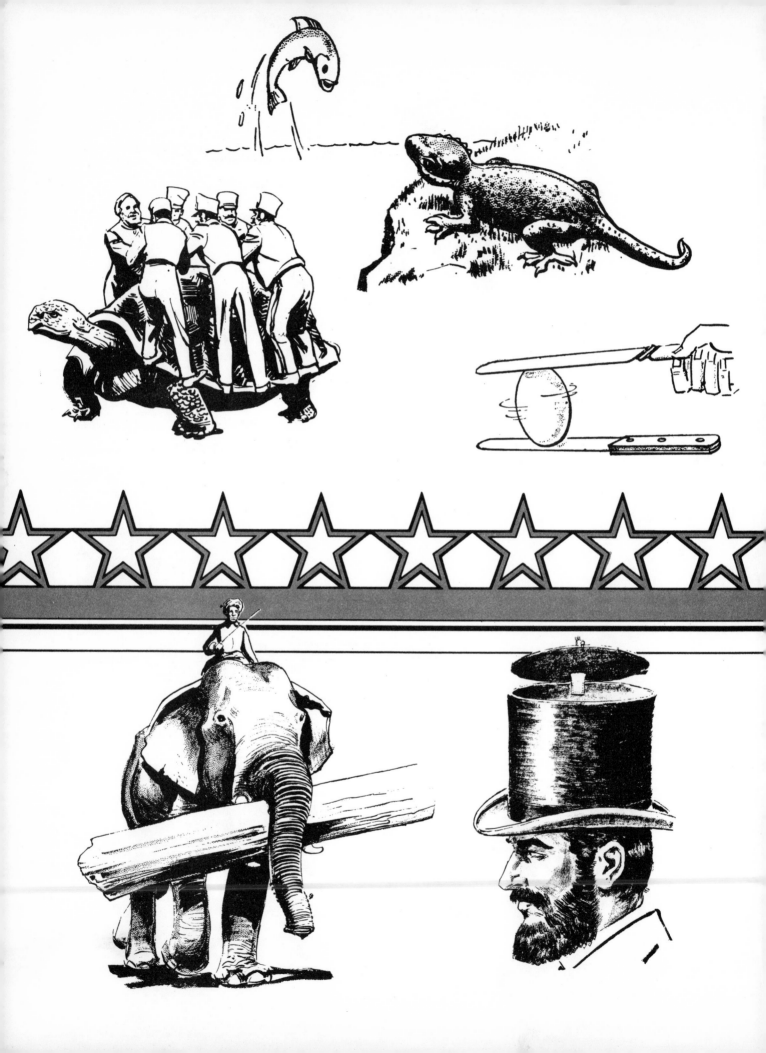

Ripley's Believe It or Not!®

Golden Press • New York

Western Publishing Company, Inc.
Racine, Wisconsin

FIRST GOLDEN PRESS EDITION

THE STRANGEST HORSE RACE IN THE WORLD !

A GRUELLING CROSS-COUNTRY RACE STAGED ANNUALLY IN MONGOLIA TO DETERMINE THE COUNTRY'S THREE FASTEST HORSES, ALWAYS HAS 200 HORSES RIDDEN MADLY OVER AN 18-MILE COURSE BY CHILDREN 5 TO 8 YEARS OF AGE !

YOUNGSTERS – MANY OF WHOM HAVE TO BE TIED ON THEIR MOUNTS – ARE USED AS JOCKEYS TO GIVE A TRUE TEST OF THE HORSE'S NATURAL ABILITY. YET IN CENTURIES THERE HAS NOT BEEN A SINGLE ACCIDENT

A **MOTHER** IN TUTIN, YUGOSLAVIA, CARRIES HER BABY IN A CRADLE ON HER HEAD --*KEEPING IT BALANCED WITH A RAKE*

THE BRIDGE THAT MAKES THE DEVIL DIZZY SHANGHAI CONSTRUCTED IN THE FAITH OF THE CHINESE TO MISLEAD THE DEVIL BY ITS ANGLES AND ZIGZAGS

The **WHIRLIGIG BEETLE** TO ESCAPE ITS SURFACE ENEMIES CRASH DIVES UNDERWATER WITH *A BUBBLE OF AIR TRAPPED BENEATH ITS WING COVERS*

WEDDING GOWNS WORN BY NOBLE WOMEN IN JAPAN, COMPRISED AS MANY AS **9** KIMONOS

5

Ripley's Believe It or Not!

THE MOST CAUTIOUS TRAVELER IN HISTORY!

SENATOR ALEXANDER SLUCHEVSKY A WEALTHY RESIDENT of Kharkov, in the Ukraine, TRAVELED BY TRAIN TO ST. PETERSBURG SEVERAL TIMES EACH YEAR —BUT HE ALWAYS RODE ON A FLAT CAR, SEATED IN HIS OWN CARRIAGE, TO WHICH WERE HITCHED A TEAM OF WHITE HORSES SO HE COULD CONTINUE HIS JOURNEY IF THE TRAIN BROKE DOWN

BICYCLE BUILT FOR 10
THE DECEMTUPLE, BUILT IN 1896, CARRIED 10 RIDERS

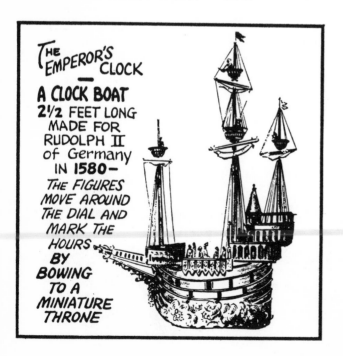

THE EMPEROR'S CLOCK — A CLOCK BOAT 2½ FEET LONG MADE FOR RUDOLPH II of Germany IN 1580 — THE FIGURES MOVE AROUND THE DIAL AND MARK THE HOURS BY BOWING TO A MINIATURE THRONE

JACK TERRY CROSSED THE ENGLISH CHANNEL FROM DOVER TO CALAIS **ON A TRICYCLE** HE MADE THE TRIP IN 8 HOURS, KEPT AFLOAT BY THE RUBBER TIRES AND STEERING WITH HIS REAR WHEEL July 28, 1883

A RAKE MADE BY AMERICAN INDIANS *FROM THE ANTLERS OF A DEER*

THE **MIGHTY MITE** Bertholdo A 2½-FOOT MIDGET, WAS PRIME MINISTER OF LOMBARDY FROM 566 TO 573 --*NEXT TO KING ALBOIN THE MIGHTIEST MAN IN THE KINGDOM*

AN **AUTOMOBILE** PATENTED IN THE U·S· IN 1911, WAS HITCHED TO A MECHANICAL HORSE WHICH *MOVED ITS LEGS REALISTICALLY*

THE **FIRST METAL-LINED BATHTUB·** WAS CONSTRUCTED BY ADAM THOMPSON OF CINCINNATI, OHIO, IN 1840, AND WEIGHED· *NEARLY A TON*

THE STRANGEST CHRISTMAS TREE
SCUBA DIVERS
IN THE ITALIAN NATIONAL UNDERSEA EXPEDITION OF 1952
CELEBRATED CHRISTMAS BY DECORATING A CORAL BUSH
WITH COLORED LIGHTS 100 FEET BELOW THE SURFACE
OF THE RED SEA

THERE ARE OVER 4,000 MAN-MADE THINGS FLYING ABOUT IN OUTER SPACE! EVEN THE SCIENTISTS WHO SENT THEM UP THERE HAVE LOST TRACK OF THEM. ONE BRITISH SATELLITE TRACKER SAYS "WE FIND ONE BIT AND LOSE ANOTHER!"

TREE LIGHTNING

ARBORESCENT LIGHTNING WHICH OCCURS ONLY DURING TROPICAL STORMS IN SOUTH AMERICA TRACES IN THE SKY THE OUTLINE OF A LEAFLESS TREE AND, UNLIKE NORMAL LIGHTNING, *ITS FLASHES ALWAYS ASCEND*

THE DAY THE SKY RAINED FIRE !

THE HEAVENS OVER NORTH AMERICA WERE LIT UP ON NOVEMBER 13, 1833, *BY 200,000 SHOOTING STARS*! NONE OF THEM REACHED THE EARTH

THE LARGEST METEORITE EVER FOUND ON EARTH FELL IN 1920 AT HOBA WEST IN SOUTHWEST AFRICA. IT WAS NINE FEET BY EIGHT FEET AND WEIGHED *132,000 POUNDS!*

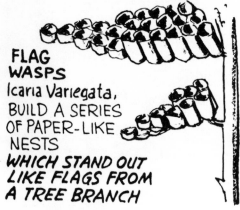

FLAG WASPS
Icaria Variegata, BUILD A SERIES OF PAPER-LIKE NESTS *WHICH STAND OUT LIKE FLAGS FROM A TREE BRANCH*

The **WHITE-THROATED WOOD RAT** ESCAPES ITS MORE TENDER-FOOTED ENEMIES BY *RUNNING OVER CACTUS SPINES*

THE CHURCH OF OSTHEIM IN ALSACE, FRANCE, WRECKED IN WORLD WAR II BOMBING RAIDS, IS PRESERVED AS A WAR MEMORIAL BECAUSE STORKS *BUILT A NEST ATOP THE RUINS*

BOYS' DAY IS CELEBRATED ANNUALLY IN JAPAN BY FLYING FOR EACH BOY IN THE HOUSEHOLD A **REPLICA OF A CARP** – *THE CARP'S DETERMINATION IN SWIMMING UPSTREAM HAS MADE IT THE SYMBOL OF RUGGED MANHOOD*

ACORN BARNACLES TO AVOID BEING EATEN BY THE DOG-WHELK *ATTACH THEMSELVES TO ITS SHELL – THE ONLY PLACE THE WHELK CANNOT REACH*

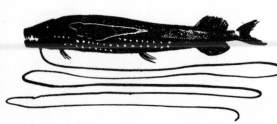

LAMPROTOXUS A DEEP-SEA FISH FOUND OFF IRELAND HAS SEVERAL ROWS OF LUMINOUS "PORTHOLES" *AND AN ANTENNA 5 TIMES AS LONG AS ITS BODY*

A **HERMIT CRAB** THAT HAS *A BOARDER AND A SERVANT* THE BOARDER IS AN ANEMONE, ATOP THE CRAB'S SHELL, AND THE SERVANT IS A NEREIS, A SEA WORM THAT LIVES INSIDE THE CRAB'S SHELL -*AND KEEPS IT CLEAN*

A **REDWOOD** IN THE ELK VALLEY CUTOFF NEAR CRESCENT CITY, CALIF., LIES ON THE GROUND AND NO LONGER HAS ROOTS--*YET 14 TREES ARE GROWING FROM IT*

A **RACCOON** WAS TRAINED BY OWEN JONES, OF STEUBEN HILLS, N.Y., TO EAT AT ITS OWNER'S TABLE, DRINK COFFEE, AND *DUNK BREAD IN COFFEE, SOUP OR LIQUOR*

HIGH-RISE BIRDHOUSE A BIRDHOUSE ERECTED BY GLEN TIMONEY, OF OAKLAND,ME., *HAS 12 "APARTMENTS" AND IS MOUNTED ON A 35- FT. HIGH POLE WHICH HAS 17 MORE "APARTMENTS"* Submitted by Jules H. Marr, Albuquerque,N.M.

CHEEP RENT BIRD'S EYE VIEW HIGH RISE APARTMENTS BIRDS ONLY

THE **WALRUS** DRAGS ITSELF OVER THE ICE BY ITS **TUSKS**

THE **CADDIS WORM** CUTS MINIATURE LOGS FROM TWIGS TO BUILD ITS SHELTER- *BOTH ENDS OF THE "HOUSE" ARE OPEN SO THE WORM CAN WALK -CARRYING ITS SHELTER WITH IT*

THE GHOST CRAB IS CREAM COLORED WHEN IT IS ON DRY SAND BUT WHEN THE SAND IS WET THE CRAB BLENDS *INTO A COMBINATION OF GRAY, PURPLE AND BROWN*

Ripley's Believe It or Not!

HOT DOGS

THE COUNTESS WILHELMINE (1709-1758) of Bayreuth, Germany, SISTER OF KING FREDERICK THE GREAT OF PRUSSIA, TO KEEP HER FEET WARM IN WINTER ALWAYS SLEPT WITH 7 DOGS *GROUPED AROUND HER FEET*

Dogs DURING THE SPRING THAW IN GREENLAND, AS PROTECTION AGAINST THE SHARP CRUST OF THE SNOW, *WEAR SEALSKIN SHOES*

KING HENRY III
(1551-1589) of France

WAS SO FOND OF PETS THAT WHENEVER HIS FAVORITE DOG HAD A LITTER *THE MONARCH WOULD CARRY THE PUPPIES FOR DAYS IN A BASKET SLUNG FROM HIS NECK*

THE **OWL** BUTTERFLY IS NOT HARMED BY PREDATORS BECAUSE ITS CAMOUFLAGE MAKES IT LOOK LIKE A **FIERCE BIRD OF PREY**

JUANITO APINANI A 19th-CENTURY MATADOR FROM SPAIN, THRILLED CROWDS BY USING A LANCE TO LEAP OVER A CHARGING BULL

THE COWFIGHTERS WHO ARE MORE COURAGEOUS THAN BULLFIGHTERS!

COWFIGHTERS, of the Landes area of southern France, FACE THE HORNS OF WILD COWS WITH NO DEFENSE WEAPON OF ANY KIND THEY MUST ESCAPE THE COW'S SHARP HORNS BY LEAPING HIGH INTO THE AIR – AND TO AVOID A HEAD-ON CHARGE *THEIR JUMP MUST CARRY THEM OVER THE FULL LENGTH OF THE COW*

THE **MEERKAT** OF So. AFRICA, APPEARS TO HAVE A SEAM FROM THE MIDDLE OF ITS CHIN DOWN THE ENTIRE LENGTH OF ITS BODY... *MAKING IT LOOK LIKE A STUFFED ANIMAL*

THE **TRUNK** OF AN ELEPHANT *IS OPERATED BY* **40,000** MUSCLES

THE **SQUIRREL** USES ITS TAIL AS A SUNSHADE, AN UMBRELLA AND A BLANKET

KAATERSKILL FALLS

IN THE CATSKILL MOUNTAINS, N.Y., 260 FEET HIGH, IS MARKED BY A MEMORIAL TABLET *TO A MONGREL TERRIER THAT LEAPED TO ITS DEATH OVER THE FALLS-* THE DOG'S MASTER HAD TOSSED A STONE INTO THE WATER AND THE TERRIER, TRAINED TO RETRIEVE ANYTHING ITS OWNER THREW, UNHESITATINGLY PLUNGED AFTER IT

THE **SAGUARO CACTUS** ATTAINS A WEIGHT OF **12** TONS AND CAN STORE UP *A TON OF WATER-* IT ANNUALLY PRODUCES 275,000 SEEDS -ONLY ONE OF WHICH EVER BECOMES A NEW PLANT

A **STONE WOLFHOUND** ON THE WALLS OF ANTRIM CASTLE, IRELAND, IS A MEMORIAL TO A WOLFHOUND THAT SAVED LADY MARION CLOTWORTHY FROM A WOLF ATTACK IN 1660 AND ALSO ALERTED THE CASTLE TO A SNEAK ONSLAUGHT BY AN ENEMY FORCE

BAOBOB TREES
FOUND IN THE TROPICS, HAVE *TRUNKS 30 FEET IN DIAMETER*

DEER WITH **78-POINT ANTLERS** SHOT NEAR BRADY, TEXAS, 1892 Buckhorn Museum, San Antonio, Texas

A **CAT** TRAILING A GROUP OF ALPINISTS FROM THE HOTEL BELVEDERE, LOCATED AT AN ALTITUDE OF 10,820 FEET ON THE MATTERHORN *CLIMBED TO THE SUMMIT - AT A HEIGHT OF 14,780 FEET* (1950)

THE **LONG-TAILED SHEEP** OF INDIA AND ASIA MINOR, PULL A SMALL 2-WHEELED CART WHICH *SUPPORTS THEIR 10-LB. TAIL*

THE CONTRADICTORY CAT
KITTEN WITH "OK" ON ONE SIDE AND "NO" ON THE OTHER - *BOTH NATURAL MARKINGS* Submitted by Mrs. Stephen E. Randall, Gouverneur, N.Y.

15

A STRIPED BARBER POLE 12 FEET HIGH, MADE FROM A CEDAR LOG, WITHSTOOD THE 1904 FIRE *THAT DESTROYED EVERY MAJOR DOWNTOWN BUILDING IN BALTIMORE, MD.*

THE WOOD THAT BURNED UNDERWATER!

A LUMBER YARD at Horsham, Australia, WAS COMPLETELY DESTROYED BY FIRE IN 1909 *ALTHOUGH THE YARD WAS DEEPLY IMMERSED BY FLOOD WATERS AND THE AREA WAS BEING SWEPT BY A TORRENTIAL RAINSTORM* LIME STORED IN THE YARD KEPT THE LUMBER BURNING FURIOUSLY

THE FROZEN WATERFALL of Mt. Beardmore, in the Antarctic HAS A HEIGHT OF MORE THAN 10,000 FEET — *60 TIMES THAT OF NIAGARA FALLS*

THE "STAINED WINDOWS" OF THE RED FORT IN DELHI, INDIA, HAVE NO GLASS AT ALL — *THE DESIGNS HAVING BEEN CARVED IN STONE*

THE TOWN WITHOUT A SINGLE STREET

Sewell
A COMMUNITY ON
El Teniente Mountain,
Chile,
HAS A POPULATION
OF 6,000 -BUT IT
HAS NO STREETS
OR VEHICLES
*ITS SIDEWALKS
CONSIST ENTIRELY
OF STAIRWAYS*

THE BAY OF IMPERNAL
Portuguese Guinea, Africa,
IS 59 FEET DEEP HALF OF EACH DAY
AND DURING THE OTHER 12 HOURS
BONE·DRY

THE FIRST DIVING BELL
FRANZ KESSLER
a German landscape painter
INVENTED A WOODEN DIVING
BELL WITH WINDOWS IN 1611
TO PAINT UNDERWATER SCENES

MOUNTAIN CLIMBERS
MUST CLAMBER UP THE STEEP CLIFFS OVERHANGING
THE ALPINE HIGHWAY, IN BAVARIA, EACH SPRING
TO DISLODGE ROCKS LOOSENED BY THE THAW

A **MAORI WAR CANOE** IN A MUSEUM IN AUCKLAND, N.Z., MEASURES 82 FEET LONG AND 6 FEET WIDE, *AND CARRIED 100 PEOPLE*

THE **WASHINGTON MONUMENT** in Washington, D.C., ON WHICH ALL WORK WAS HALTED FOR A PERIOD OF 20 YEARS, WAS DESCRIBED BY MARK TWAIN IN 1873 AS LOOKING LIKE " *A FACTORY CHIMNEY WITH THE TOP BROKEN OFF* "

ICEBERGS WHOSE BOTTOMS HAVE BEEN ERODED BY THE SEA WATER, SOMETIMES IMPERIL PASSING SHIPS BY SUDDENLY *TURNING UPSIDE DOWN*

THE **COPPER WEATHER VANE** OVER THE LIBERTY & CO. STORE IN London, England, *IS A 120-LB. REPLICA OF THE MAYFLOWER*

A **LETTER** MAILED BY EMANUEL EHRLICH OF JACKSONVILLE, FLA., IN MAY, 1942, WAS RETURNED TO HIM AS UNDELIVERABLE BY THE U.S. POSTAL SERVICE **29 YEARS LATER** Submitted by E. Ehrlich

THE **SAILS** OF NATIVE FISHING CANOES on Wagifa Island, New Guinea, ARE MADE BY SEWING TOGETHER *LEAVES OF THE SAGO PALM*

FRED BALDASARE
of Cocoa, Florida,
SWAM THE ENGLISH
CHANNEL, COVERING A
DISTANCE OF **42 MILES,**
ENTIRELY UNDERWATER
July 10-11, 1962

CATALONIAN FISHERMEN
SPREAD THEIR NETS
AT NIGHT AND
ATTRACT THE FISH
TO THEIR BOATS
**BY USE OF GIANT
ARC LIGHTS**

A
**GIANT
REDWOOD
TREE**
CONTAINS
MORE
WATER
THAN
WOOD !

A TRUNK
200 FEET
HIGH
HOLDS
**4,700
GALLONS**

THE
**BOUNCING
BOATS OF
MADRAS**
India
The **MASULLAH,** A BOAT MADE OF
THIN PLANKS TIED TOGETHER
WITH COCONUT FIBERS, IS SO
ELASTIC THAT WHEN CRUSHED
IN COLLISION, *IT ALWAYS
BOUNCES BACK INTO ITS
PROPER SHAPE WITHOUT
DAMAGE*

THE **SEEDS** of the
SWARTZIA TREE,
in the jungles
of Dutch Guiana,
DANGLE AS HIGH
AS 90 FEET
IN THE AIR - AT
*THE END OF
SPRINGLIKE
THREADS 10
FEET LONG*

Ripley's Believe It or Not!

THE **SHELL** OF AN OSTRICH EGG IS USED AS A **WATER PITCHER** In Africa

A **MUSTACHE PROTECTOR** DEVISED BY ELI J.F. RANDOLPH, OF N.Y., IN 1872, WAS A HARD-RUBBER DEVICE WITH PRONGS THAT FITTED INTO THE NOSTRILS TO KEEP *THE MUSTACHE DRY WHEN EATING AND DRINKING*

John Hancock

WAS THE ONLY ONE OF THE **56** SIGNERS OF THE DECLARATION OF INDEPENDENCE **WHO ACTUALLY SIGNED IT ON JULY 4th!**

52 OF THEM AFFIXED THEIR SIGNATURES AUG. 2, 1776 AND THE OTHERS SIGNED IT LATER-- ONE OF THEM IN 1781

THE **KIWI BIRD** New Zealand **RESTS BY LEANING ON ITS BEAK!**

SHOE In Tibet **WITH A BUILT-IN SHOE HORN**

COWBOYS IN TEXAS IN THE 1830s, WERE ORIGINALLY CALLED "COWHUNTERS" --*BUT THE NAME WAS CHANGED BECAUSE OF THEIR YOUTH*

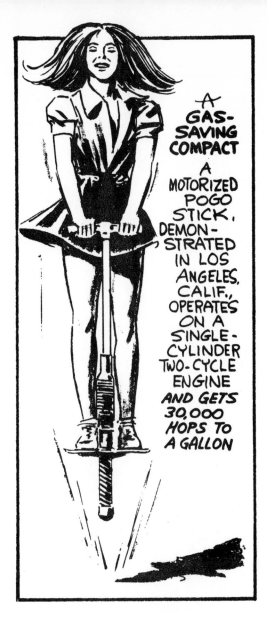

A GAS-SAVING COMPACT

A MOTORIZED POGO STICK, DEMONSTRATED IN LOS ANGELES, CALIF., OPERATES ON A SINGLE-CYLINDER TWO-CYCLE ENGINE *AND GETS 30,000 HOPS TO A GALLON*

THE DESERT HUTS THAT PROVIDE BREAKFAST IN BED

BEDOUINS BUILD THEIR HOMES IN THE SAHARA AROUND A LIVE DATE PALM —*AND EACH MORNING FIND ON THEIR BED SUFFICIENT FRUIT FOR THEIR MORNING MEAL*

THE RING THAT WAS RETURNED BY A FISH!

MADAME EDUIGUE REREIT, of Paris, France, LOST HER RING WHILE WORKING IN HER KITCHEN AND RECOVERED IT A FEW DAYS LATER FROM *A FISH SHE HAD BOUGHT IN THE PUBLIC MARKET*

THE RING HAD SLID DOWN THE KITCHEN DRAIN, BEEN WASHED INTO THE RIVER -- AND WAS SWALLOWED BY A FISH THAT WAS PURCHASED BY MADAME REREIT HERSELF IN THE MOST AMAZING EXAMPLE OF COINCIDENCE, IN MODERN TIMES (1903)

21

BARON CHRISTOPHE de TURSANNE
of Bigorres, France,
WHEN HIS PONY BECAME LAME IN
A HUNTING ACCIDENT, CARRIED THE 420-LB.
ANIMAL TO A VETERINARIAN ON HIS
OWN SHOULDERS – A DISTANCE
OF 1¼ MILES!

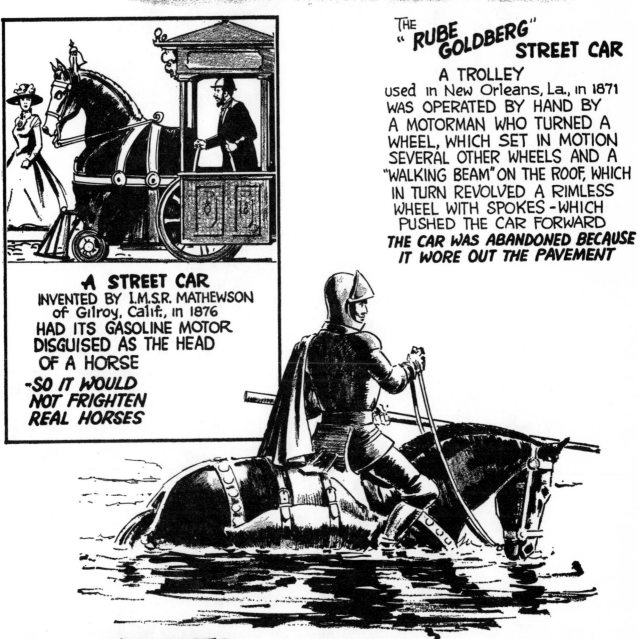

THE "RUBE GOLDBERG" STREET CAR

A TROLLEY used in New Orleans, La., in 1871 WAS OPERATED BY HAND BY A MOTORMAN WHO TURNED A WHEEL, WHICH SET IN MOTION SEVERAL OTHER WHEELS AND A "WALKING BEAM" ON THE ROOF, WHICH IN TURN REVOLVED A RIMLESS WHEEL WITH SPOKES – WHICH PUSHED THE CAR FORWARD

THE CAR WAS ABANDONED BECAUSE IT WORE OUT THE PAVEMENT

A STREET CAR
INVENTED BY I.M.S.R. MATHEWSON of Gilroy, Calif., in 1876 HAD ITS GASOLINE MOTOR DISGUISED AS THE HEAD OF A HORSE

– SO IT WOULD NOT FRIGHTEN REAL HORSES

KNIGHTS in medieval times OFTEN FLOATED ACROSS LAKES AND STREAMS BY ATTACHING TO THE FLANKS OF THEIR HORSES *INFLATED GOAT SKINS*

THE EYE OF HORUS, an ancient Egyptian divinity THAT WAS A SYMBOL OF PROTECTION AND HEALING, IS THE SOURCE OF THE SIGN USED BY MODERN PHYSICIANS ON PRESCRIPTIONS -- R_x

BIG TREE STUMP DANCE FLOOR OF CALAVERAS COUNTY, California

COTILLION PARTY OF 49 PERSONS DANCED ON THE STUMP OF THE MAMMOTH SEQUOIA TREE
THE ORIGINAL TREE WAS *302 FEET HIGH AND 2000 YEARS OLD*! 1854

A **HOUSE** IN KAMALA NEHRU PARK, IN BOMBAY, INDIA, *SHAPED LIKE A GIANT SHOE*

TY COBB WHO IN 1913 WAS THE HIGHEST-SALARIED OUTFIELDER IN BASEBALL, *WAS PAID $12,000 A YEAR*

A **SINGLE GIANT ROLL** BAKED IN 1730 TO FEED THE SAXON ARMY ON MANEUVERS NEAR RADEWITZ, WAS 28 FEET LONG, 12 FEET WIDE, HAULED BY 8 HORSES AND *CUT WITH A KNIFE 20 FEET LONG*

THE BUTTERFLY BOATS OF AFRICA

THE FISHING VESSELS of the Kotokos of the Chari River HAVE WINGS FASHIONED FROM FISHING NETS —*IN THE BELIEF IT GIVES THEM GREATER SPEED*— THE BOATS ARE MADE OF WOODEN PLANKS —**SEWN TOGETHER WITH VEGETABLE VINES**

THE FEATHERED "BIRD DOG"

THE CAGOU, A BIRD FOUND ONLY ON THE ISLAND OF NEW CALEDONIA, *CANNOT FLY AND BARKS LIKE A DOG*

DEBORAH SAMPSON — Plympton, Mass.

THE ONLY U.S. WOMAN SOLDIER OFFICIALLY ACKNOWLEDGED BY THE U.S. GOVERNMENT AND AN ACT OF CONGRESS!

SHE ENLISTED IN THE CONTINENTAL ARMY, TOOK PART IN ALL ENGAGEMENTS AND WAS WOUNDED TWICE.

CONGRESS AWARDED HER A PENSION

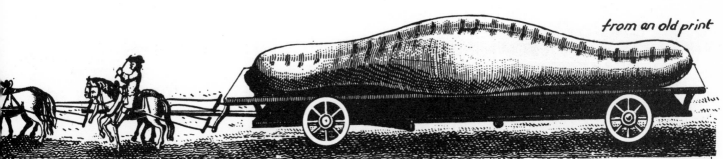

from an old print

Lincoln AND NUMBER 7

EACH NAME CONTAINS 7 LETTERS.
LIVED 7 YRS IN KENTUCKY AND 7 YRS IN SALEM.
HE WAS A **PRIVATE** (7 LETTERS) AND A **CAPTAIN**
(7 LETTERS), ELECTED 7 TIMES—SWORN INTO CONGRESS
DEC 7, 1847, HELD 7 OFFICES IN SUCCESSION IN SPRINGFIELD.
7 VOTES WERE CAST AGAINST HIM IN THE ELECTION OF 1832,
HAD 7 DEBATES WITH **STEPHEN DOUGLAS** (TWICE 7 LETTERS),
FOUGHT **SLAVERY** (7 LETTERS).
ANCESTORS CAME FROM **HINGHAM** (7 LETTERS), **ENGLAND** (7 LETTERS),
COUNTY OF **NORWICH** (7 LETTERS), MOVED AT THE AGE OF 7 TO **SPENCER**
(7 LETTERS), **INDIANA** (7 LETTERS), WAS 7 YEARS IN STATE LEGISLATURE—APPOINTED
7 CABINET MINISTERS—7 STATES SECEDED.   HIS BEST GENERAL WAS **U.S. GRANT**
(7 LETTERS) AND HE **DIED** A FEW MINUTES AFTER 7 ON THE 7 TH DAY

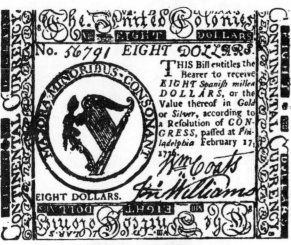

THE 8-DOLLAR BILL!

DESIGNED AND PRINTED BY BENJAMIN FRANKLIN FOR THE AMERICAN COLONIES

THE WORST-DRESSED WOMEN IN THE WORLD

A WOMAN OF THE TODA TRIBE OF SOUTHERN INDIA, GETS ONLY **2** GARMENTS THROUGHOUT HER ENTIRE LIFETIME

SHE IS GIVEN ONE IN CHILDHOOD, AND THE SECOND WHEN SHE IS MARRIED

Abigail SMITH

WAS THE <u>WIFE</u> OF A PRESIDENT
AND THE <u>MOTHER</u> OF A PRESIDENT

(John Adams – John Quincy Adams)

27

Ripley's Believe It or Not!

A **MONASTERY** BUILT ON A HIGH ROCK NEAR ADUWA, ETHIOPIA, CAN BE REACHED ONLY BY *A ROPE LOWERED DOWN THE SHEER CLIFF*

CAPTAIN HERMAN LEMAIRE AFTER LOSING A LEG IN THE NAPOLEONIC RETREAT FROM MOSCOW, DELIVERED SECRET DISPATCHES TO NAPOLEON BY DRESSING HIMSELF IN BEGGAR'S CLOTHING AND, ON A HASTILY FITTED WOODEN LEG, *WALKING FROM HAMBURG, GERMANY, TO PARIS, FRANCE, A DISTANCE OF 600 MILES* (1812)

THE STONE GATE

ON THE ROAD BETWEEN WEGGIS AND KALTBAD, SWITZERLAND, WAS FORMED BY 4 HUGE ROCKS THAT ROLLED DOWN THE MOUNTAIN –AND FORMED A PERFECT GATEWAY

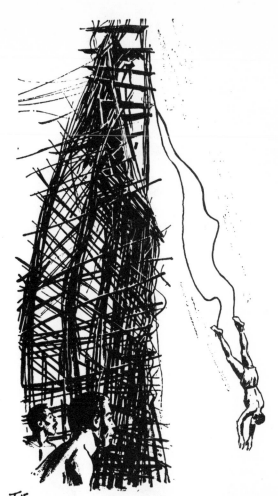

THE DARING LAND DIVERS OF PENTECOST
New Hebrides

NATIVES DIVE HEADLONG FROM A TOWER 80 FEET HIGH, WITH LIGHT ROPES OF VINES ATTACHED TO THEIR ANKLES

THE ROPES BREAK DURING THE JUMP –BUT CHECK THEIR PLUNGE JUST ENOUGH TO PERMIT THEM TO FALL UNHARMED

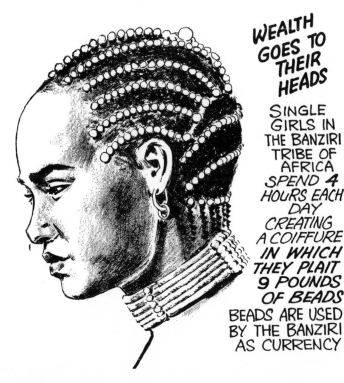

WEALTH GOES TO THEIR HEADS

SINGLE GIRLS IN THE BANZIRI TRIBE OF AFRICA SPEND 4 HOURS EACH DAY CREATING A COIFFURE IN WHICH THEY PLAIT 9 POUNDS OF BEADS

BEADS ARE USED BY THE BANZIRI AS CURRENCY

TIBETAN PONIES AT OVERNIGHT CAMPS ON FROZEN LAKE PHARIA OBTAIN WATER BY DIGGING HOLES IN THE ICE WITH THEIR HOOVES

29

Ripley's Believe It or Not!

FENCES in the Faroes Islands, Denmark, ARE STILL MADE FROM THE SKULLS OF DOLPHINS

PLAYING CARDS used in France in the 19th century IN WHICH THE FACES CHANGED WHEN THE CARDS WERE INVERTED

THE NECKLACED LAUGHING THRUSH of India DISPLAYS ON ITS BREAST WHAT APPEARS TO BE A NECKLACE OF BLACK PEARLS

THE ELEPHANT THAT DEFEATED AN ARMY India "GULAM ALI"

a military elephant in the Moslem army WON THE BATTLE OF TALIKOTA IN **1565** BY WINDING ITS TRUNK AROUND THE ENEMY COMMANDER **AND HOLDING HIM CAPTIVE IN THE AIR UNTIL HIS TROOPS SURRENDERED**

WHEN THE ELEPHANT DIED YEARS LATER AN ELABORATE TOMB WAS ERECTED FOR IT IN AHMADNAGAR

JIMMY CERTAIN of Fort Lauderdale, Fla., WHO WAS CRIPPLED BY POLIO AS A CHILD, "WALKED" 50 YARDS BALANCED ON HIS HANDS IN 27 SECONDS

Submitted by Jules Henry Marr, Albuquerque, N.M.

THE **PAPER NEST** of the Brazilian wasp LOOKS AND SWINGS LIKE A JAPANESE LANTERN – ACTUALLY IT IS A MINIATURE SKYSCRAPER, COMPRISING 20 OR MORE STORIES

17-YEAR LOCUSTS ACTUALLY REQUIRE 17 YEARS TO DEVELOP -- YET, AS ADULTS, LIVE ONLY 30 TO 40 DAYS

THE JOCKEY WHO CHANGED HORSES IN THE MIDDLE OF A RACE!
MICHAEL MORRISSEY
British steeplechaser
THROWN BY ONE HORSE AT A JUMP
LANDED IN THE SADDLE OF ANOTHER
Southwell Race Track
Oct. 15, 1953

A LARGE MECHANICAL CAT IS LOCATED IN THE WINDOW OF MANY RESTAURANTS IN TOKYO, JAPAN -- A MOVING ARM BECKONING PASSERSBY TO ENTER

Ripley's Believe It or Not!

FENCES in Tibau, Brazil, ARE MADE FROM THE VEINS OF THE LEAVES **OF THE COCONUT PALM**

THE **HUTS** OF THE AFRICAN ZULUS HAVE DOORWAYS SO LOW THAT **THEY MUST BE ENTERED AND LEFT ON ALL FOURS**

THE **DEVIL PATROLMAN** WHO KEEPS ORDER IN KOLAHUN, LIBERIA, CONVINCES NATIVES HE HAS SUPER-NATURAL POWERS, BY PATROLLING THE JUNGLE PATHS ON STILTS -- **WEARING A MASK WITH NO EYE-SLITS**

NATIVES of Nimule, on the border between Uganda and Egypt, STILL FISH AS DID THEIR ANCESTORS 5,000 YEARS AGO **-- WITH BOW AND ARROW**

WILLIAM CORBETT OF RENTON, WASHINGTON, BY KARATE CHOPS WITH HIS BARE HANDS IN A PERIOD OF 17 HOURS, *SHATTERED 5,000 BRICKS*

GIRLS OF THE MANIDE TRIBE OF THE PHILIPPINES *CARRY THEIR HANDBAGS SUSPENDED FROM A COMB FASTENED IN THEIR HAIR*

THE **FEATHER GAME** IS AN ANCIENT CHINESE SPORT IN WHICH THE PLAYER IS REQUIRED TO TRANSFER A FEATHER FROM THE SOLE OF HIS FOOT *TO THE TOP OF HIS HEAD*

33

THE MOST HEROIC NAUTICAL RESCUE IN ALL HISTORY!

CAPT. THOMAS A. SCOTT BROUGHT HIS TUG ALONGSIDE A FERRYBOAT SINKING IN NEW YORK'S NORTH RIVER WITH HUNDREDS OF WOMEN AND CHILDREN ABOARD AND PLUGGED A HOLE IN THE LISTING BOAT AT THE WATER LINE WITH *HIS OWN BODY!*
CAPT. SCOTT'S ARM, WHICH PROTRUDED THROUGH THE HOLE, WAS SEVERELY LACERATED BY ICE CAKES -- *BUT ALL ABOARD THE VESSEL WERE SAVED*
January 30, 1870

KNIFE BLADES WERE MADE BY THE ANCIENT INDIANS OF HUDSON BAY *FROM THE TEETH OF BEAVERS*

TOM CALDWELL BECAME THE REGULAR U.S. MAIL CARRIER BETWEEN FORT SCOTT AND OSAGE MISSION, Kansas - RIDING 40 MILES ON HORSEBACK EACH TRIP
WHEN HE WAS ONLY 12 YEARS OF AGE
(1858)

THE SECRETARY BIRD CAN SWALLOW A HEN'S EGG WHOLE -- *WITHOUT BREAKING THE SHELL*

YAKUT TRIBESMEN in Siberia GO BEAR HUNTING *ARMED ONLY WITH A HATCHET*— IF THEY FAIL TO KILL THE BEAR THEY "PLAY DEAD" TO GAIN ANOTHER CHANCE AT THE ANIMAL

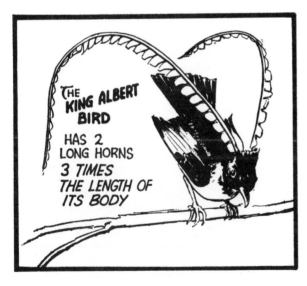

THE **KING ALBERT BIRD** HAS 2 LONG HORNS *3 TIMES THE LENGTH OF ITS BODY*

MANY TYPES OF DESERT ANTS CARRY THEIR DEAD TO ANT CEMETERIES

THE **BEAUTY** WHO BECAME A PUBLIC ATTRACTION BY CITY ORDINANCE *Paule Viguier* (1518-1610) of TOULOUSE, FRANCE, WAS SO BEAUTIFUL THAT WHEN SHE REMAINED INDOORS FOR SEVERAL DAYS *THE POPULACE RIOTED!* THE CITY ADOPTED A LAW REQUIRING HER TO APPEAR ON HER BALCONY TWICE EACH DAY--WHICH SHE DID UNTIL HER DEATH AT THE AGE OF **92**

Ripley's Believe It or Not!

AMERICAN INDIANS STALKING DEER OFTEN DISGUISED THEMSELVES *BY DONNING THE SKIN, HEAD AND ANTLERS OF A DEER*

THE **HALF DIME** MINTED IN 1792 *WAS THE FIRST U.S. COIN*

THE **AMERICAN INDIANS** DID NOT ALL SPEAK THE SAME LANGUAGE. MORE THAN 133 LANGUAGES ARE KNOWN TO HAVE BEEN USED BY THE MANY TRIBES IN VARIOUS PARTS OF THE COUNTRY.

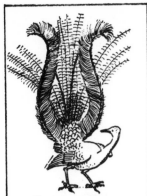

THE LYRE BIRD IS A LIAR
ITS SONGS AND CRIES ARE IMPERSONATIONS OF THOSE OF OTHER BIRDS

FOOTRACES
IN 16th CENTURY JAPAN, WERE STAGED BY ATHLETES WHO *RAN WHILE CLINGING TO THE BRIDLES OF GALLOPING HORSES*

A PHEASANT CAN EXIST WITHOUT EATING FOR **AN ENTIRE MONTH**

SAUNAS WERE VISITED BY MANY AMERICAN INDIAN TRIBES BEFORE HUNTING TRIPS IN THE BELIEF THAT IT WOULD SO CLEANSE THEM THAT ANIMALS *WOULD BE UNABLE TO DISCERN THEIR SCENT*

JOHN ADAMS (1812-1860) A HERMIT OF CALIFORNIA'S SIERRA NEVADA MTS., CAPTURED GRIZZLY BEARS AND TAMED *THEM TO SERVE AS PACK ANIMALS*

THE CORMORANT WEIGHS FROM 6 TO 8 POUNDS— YET IT EATS **15 POUNDS** OF FISH A DAY

37

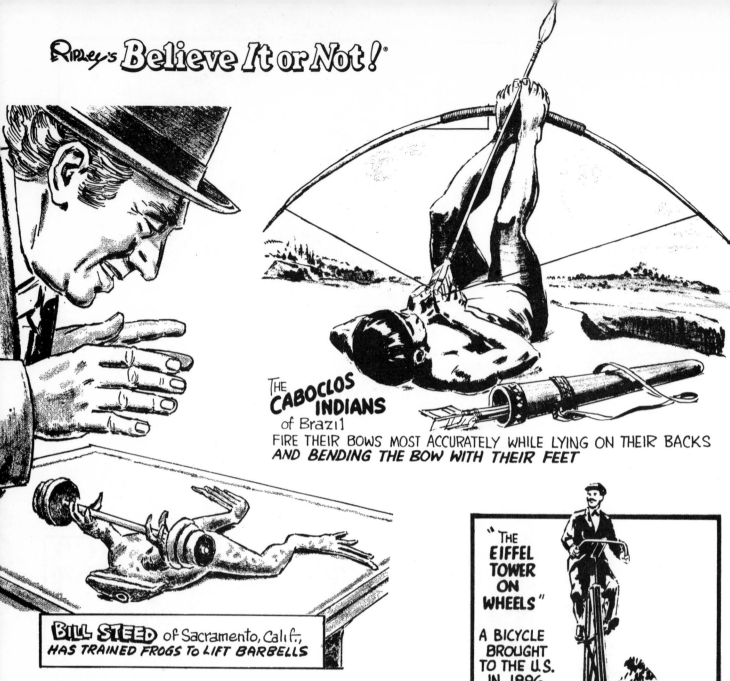

THE **CABOCLOS INDIANS** of Brazil
FIRE THEIR BOWS MOST ACCURATELY WHILE LYING ON THEIR BACKS *AND BENDING THE BOW WITH THEIR FEET*

BILL STEED of Sacramento, Calif., *HAS TRAINED FROGS TO LIFT BARBELLS*

THE BATHTUB
USED IN THE WHITE HOUSE BY PRESIDENT WILLIAM HOWARD TAFT, WAS SO HUGE, TO HOLD HIS HEFTY BULK, THAT *4 WORKMEN ONCE SAT IN IT COMFORTABLY*

"THE EIFFEL TOWER ON WHEELS"

A BICYCLE BROUGHT TO THE U.S. IN 1896 HAD A SEAT 20 FEET ABOVE THE GROUND

THE BULLDOG ANT
OF AUSTRALIA
IS AN EXCELLENT
SWIMMER AND ENJOYS
A DAILY BATH

THAT'S USING YOUR HEAD!
JOHANN SCHMITT-BLANK (1824-1880)
PROFESSOR OF CLASSICAL LANGUAGES AT
THE UNIVERSITY OF FREIBURG, GERMANY,
KEPT HIMSELF COOL ON HOT DAYS
*BY WEARING A HIGH HAT
WITH A LID THAT COULD BE
RAISED OR LOWERED BY A
WIRE THAT EXTENDED
TO HIS POCKET*

"LONG JOSEPH" SCHIPPERS
A MERRY-GO-ROUND
MANUFACTURER
OF HAMBURG,
GERMANY,
THE TALLEST
SOLDIER IN
WORLD WAR I
*MEASURED
8 FEET*

JOHANN GEORG LAHNER
1772-1840
the Viennese
butcher who
invented
frankfurters
in 1805
*ATE THEM
3 TIMES A
DAY FOR
THE LAST
35 YEARS
OF HIS
LIFE!*

THE HUMAN CANNONBALL WHO COULD NOT BE KILLED!
ARUNA, AN INDIAN HOLY MAN, WHO INCENSED THE SULTAN OF MYSORE BY
REFUSING TO BLESS A NEW GIANT MORTAR, WAS TWICE STUFFED INTO
THE BIG GUN'S BARREL AND FIRED INTO THE AIR, AND
BOTH TIMES ESCAPED UNHARMED!

THE FIRST TIME HE WAS BLOWN 800 FEET AND LANDED ON THE SOFT
CANOPY ATOP AN ELEPHANT, AND THE SECOND TIME HE FELL WITHOUT
A SCRATCH ON THE THATCHED ROOF OF A HUT   (1782)

THE PANDANGO sa LLAW
A LIVELY PHILIPPINE DANCE MUST BE PERFORMED WITH A GLASS FULL OF WATER BALANCED ON THE HEAD
-YET NOT A DROP CAN BE SPILLED

JIM SAINSBURY porter in London's Covent Garden Market BALANCED 20 BASKETS ON HIS HEAD!

LADIES IN 16th AND 17th CENTURY ENGLAND, WORE THEIR WEDDING RING ON THEIR THUMB

WHERE MASKS ARE A MUST

WOMEN OF DUBAI, ON THE PERSIAN GULF, CAN NEVER APPEAR ON THE STREET WITHOUT A BLACK·MASK

GEORGE STILLMAN OF NEW YORK CITY, TO DEMONSTRATE AMERICAN AWARENESS OF PHYSICAL FITNESS, RAN 52½ MILES ON JAN. 16, 1977 WHILE THE TEMPERATURE HOVERED AS LOW AS 7 DEGREES ABOVE ZERO

ESKIMO ICE CREAM CALLED "CACPATOK" CONSISTS OF A MIXTURE OF EDIBLE GREENS, SEAL OIL, REINDEER FAT AND SNOW

An ICICLE 200 FEET LONG HAS EXISTED FOR YEARS IN THE CLEFT OF A RED SANDSTONE WALL in the Great Gold Valley of China. *IT IS 10,000 FEET ABOVE SEA LEVEL AND NEVER WARMED BY THE SUN*

THE **SHIPWRECKED** **CREW THAT SAILED TO SAFETY ON AN ICEBERG**

19 SAILORS, WHO SURVIVED WHEN THE "U.S. POLARIS" WAS CRUSHED BY ICE IN THE ARCTIC, WERE RESCUED IN GOOD HEALTH OFF THE COAST OF LABRADOR *AFTER THEY HAD DRIFTED 1,200 MILES AND FOR 196 DAYS ON AN ICEBERG!* (Oct. 15, 1872 - April 30, 1873)

A TON OF HAY

A RANCHER VITALLY NEEDED IN SNOWBOUND SILVERTON, COLO., TO FEED HIS CATTLE, WAS MAILED FROM DURANGO BY PARCEL POST

THE HAY WAS WRAPPED IN SMALL PACKAGES AND CARRIED OVER THE MOUNTAIN TRAILS ON PACK MULES FOR $14 IN POSTAGE —BUT IT COST THE POST OFFICE $100 TO HIRE THE MULES!

(1932)

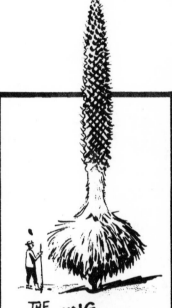

THE LIVING TORCHES

PUYA RAIMONDI — ONE OF THE EARTH'S OLDEST PLANTS— WHICH GROWS IN THE CORDILLERA MOUNTAINS OF PERU AND HAS A SHAFT OF BLOSSOMS 33 FEET HIGH, IS SO SATURATED WITH RESIN THAT SHEPHERDS LIGHT IT TO ILLUMINATE THE COUNTRYSIDE

THE WHIRLING CLOUD of MOUNT JIRINAJ (Indonesia)

A FLAT CLOUD

HOVERING OVER THE PEAK OF AN EXTINCT VOLCANO AFFECTED BY HOT AIR RISING FROM THE CRATER, SPINS SWIFTLY AROUND AND AROUND

ESKIMOS OF THE TAIMYR PENINSULA, ARCTIC SIBERIA, USE THEIR SLEDS THROUGHOUT THE SUMMER THAW BECAUSE THE RUNNERS, MADE FOR SNOW, WORK WELL ON THE MOSSY TUNDRA

AZTEC WARRIORS of Mexico FOUGHT IN LEATHER ARMOR SHAPED TO MAKE THEM *LOOK LIKE COYOTES*

JUDGES in the Dan Tribe of Liberia ARE FORBIDDEN TO HAND DOWN DECISIONS *UNLESS THEY ARE MASKED*

THE MASONRY COFFIN OF A LADY BURIED IN REGGIO, ITALY, AND EXCAVATED 2,300 YEARS LATER *WAS IN THE SHAPE OF A SCULPTURED FOOT AND SANDAL*

THE **HORNBILL** PROTECTS ITS MATE AND THEIR EGGS BY *HIDING THEM IN A HOLLOW TREE AND PLASTERING MUD OVER THE ONLY ENTRANCE* — A TINY SLIT IS LEFT THROUGH WHICH THE HORNBILL PASSES FOOD TO ITS MATE

A **NATIVE MOTHER**
in the Sudan
SIMULTANEOUSLY CARRIES
WATER FROM THE WELL
*AND GIVES HER BABY
A COLD SHOWER*

THE **RUFESCENT HOUSE WREN**
(Troglodytes musculus)
of South America
TO FEED
ITS YOUNG
*MAKES AS MANY AS
1,200 FLIGHTS FROM
ITS NEST DURING
THE DAYLIGHT HOURS
OF A SINGLE DAY*

THE **MOST ELABORATE
CROWN IN THE WORLD!**
A LANGO CHIEF
in Tanganyika, East Africa,
AS HIS BADGE OF OFFICE,
WEARS A HAIRDO THAT REQUIRES
5 YEARS TO COMPLETE.

THE CHIEF HAS COLORED WOOL
AND TUFTS OF FEATHERS WOVEN INTO
HIS HAIR—*AND HE MUST RENEW
THEM EVERY 3 MONTHS*

THE **PURSES THAT ARE
NEVER STOLEN**
THE PURSES
CARRIED BY NATIVES
of New Caledonia
ARE MADE OF WOOD IN THE
SHAPE OF A BOAT AND
*ARE TABOO TO ANYONE
BUT THEIR OWNER*

THE **KIMBERLEY DIAMOND MINE**
South Africa
IS THE LARGEST MAN-MADE HOLE IN
THE WORLD--4000 FT. DEEP AND
1,500 FT. IN CIRCUMFERENCE

THE **FRILLED LIZARD**
of Australia,
FRIGHTENS OFF
PREDATORS BY
REARING UP AND
UNFOLDING A
MANTLE **9** INCHES
IN DIAMETER

DEWITT CLINTON AS MAYOR OF NEW YORK CITY, IN 1814, WHEN THE BRITISH HAD BURNED THE CAPITOL AND WHITE HOUSE IN WASHINGTON, D.C., ARRANGED TO LOAN THE GOVERNMENT OF THE UNITED STATES $1,000,000

GREATEST RIDE
IN ALL HISTORY

SAM DALE, PIONEER SCOUT **RODE 1000 MILES IN 14½ DAYS USING ONLY 2 HORSES**

HE CARRIED A MESSAGE FROM MILLEDGEVILLE, GEORGIA TO ANDREW JACKSON IN NEW ORLEANS. HE RETURNED IMMEDIATELY ON ANOTHER HORSE AND RODE TO FORT DECATUR—1814

ED SCHIEFFELIN A PROSPECTOR IN SOUTHERN ARIZONA IN THE 1870's, WARNED THAT HE WAS MORE APT TO FIND A TOMBSTONE THAN RICHES, *NAMED THE MINE HE FOUND TOMBSTONE.*

IT YIELDED $40,000,000 IN SILVER AND $3,000,000 IN GOLD

PICTURE OF A DEER in the Buckhorn Museum, in San Antonio, Texas, *CREATED FROM THE RATTLES OF 637 RATTLESNAKES*

The LONG FURROW

LYMAN DILLON

PLOWED A FURROW 100 MILES LONG!
FROM IOWA CITY TO DUBUQUE
1839
TO ESTABLISH A GUIDE FOR STRANGERS
GOING TO THE SEAT OF GOVERNMENT OF IOWA
This Furrow is Now A Highway

GENERAL ZACHARY TAYLOR

ALMOST LOST THE NOMINATION
FOR PRESIDENT OF THE U.S.
WHEN THE LETTER ASKING
HIM TO ACCEPT THE HONOR
WAS RETURNED UNOPENED
BY TAYLOR BECAUSE IT
CAME "**POSTAGE COLLECT**"

THE FIRST MOVIE STAR!
FRED OTT, AN AIDE IN
THOMAS ALVA EDISON'S
LAB IN WEST ORANGE, N.J.,
GAVE THE FIRST MOVING
PERFORMANCE IN FILM
HISTORY--*A SNEEZE*
-1893-

RIPLey's **Believe It or Not!**

THE AMAZING HIGH DIVERS OF CAPE DUKATO
Island of Leukas, Greece

YOUNG PRIESTS, TO QUALIFY FOR SERVICE AT THE TEMPLE OF APOLLO, WERE REQUIRED IN ANCIENT GREECE TO DON THE WINGS OF AN EAGLE AND PLUNGE FROM THE CAPE INTO THE SEA -**A DIVE OF 230 FEET!**

IT WAS ASSUMED THE GODS WOULD ELIMINATE THOSE UNFIT – BUT NO DIVER WAS EVER INJURED, ALTHOUGH THE ORDEAL WAS PERFORMED FOR CENTURIES

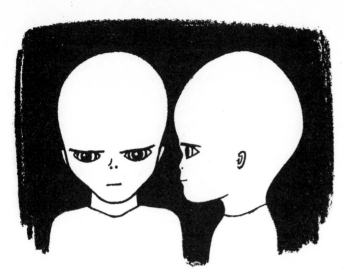

2 MEN... AIR FORCE SGT. CHARLES L. MOODY AND TRAVIS WALTON... BOTH CLAIMED TO HAVE MET CREATURES FROM OUTER SPACE! THEY DREW AMAZINGLY SIMILAR PICTURES - OF THE VERY SAME CREATURE ... <u>YET THEY NEVER MET EACH OTHER</u>!

THE LAND OF **5** SUNS

EARLY MORNING MISTS near Sing-nying-chu, China, CREATE AS AN OPTICAL ILLUSION IN THE SKY **5 SUNS**

ACCORDING TO THE GALLUP POLL... OVER **5,000,000** AMERICANS CLAIM TO HAVE ACTUALLY SEEN A UFO. AND NEARLY **HALF** OF THE POPULATION BELIEVES IN THEIR EXISTENCE!

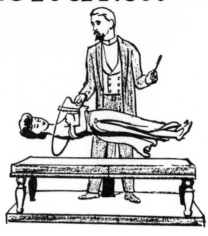

A MECHANICAL TOY CREATED FOR THE YOUNG SON OF GUILLOTINED KING LOUIS XVI of France COMPRISES A DOLL LYING ON A BENCH FANNING HERSELF-BUT SUDDENLY SHE FLOATS INTO THE AIR WITHOUT VISIBLE SUPPORT SO THAT A RING CAN BE PASSED COMPLETELY AROUND HER

A COPPER TOKEN WORTH 18 CENTS, WAS AN HOUR'S PAY IN THE HARZ SECTION OF GERMANY

FOR PUSHING A MINE CART LOADED WITH COAL

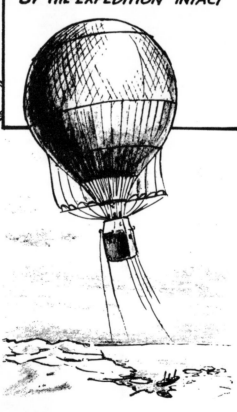

A BALLOON IN WHICH SWEDISH EXPLORER S.A. ANDRÉE AND 2 COMPANIONS TOOK OFF FROM SPITZBERGEN TO THE NORTH POLE IN 1897, WAS FOUND 33 YEARS LATER PERFECTLY PRESERVED BENEATH THE ARCTIC ICE --*WITH EVEN PHOTOGRAPHS TAKEN BY THE EXPEDITION INTACT*

BLONDIN A FRENCH TIGHTROPE WALKER, CROSSED NIAGARA RIVER ON AUGUST 17, 1859, *CARRYING A MAN NAMED HENRY COLCORD ON HIS BACK*

ALEXANDER DUMAS (1802-1870) celebrated French novelist BECAUSE HE ALWAYS WALKED ON TIPTOES AS A CHILD AND SEEMED ABOUT TO SOAR AWAY *WAS FORCED BY HIS MOTHER TO* **WEAR SHOES OF SOLID IRON**

THE **WORLD'S CHAMPION SOMERSAULTER** RAINER KUHN of Gatlinburg, Tenn., *PERFORMED 326 CONTINUOUS SOMERSAULTS ON A TRAMPOLINE.* Old Heidelberg Castle, Gatlinburg - Aug. 13, 1977

TUMBLE DOLLS WERE ORIGINATED BY THE CHINESE WHO MADE THEM IN THE IMAGE OF BUDDHA WITH WEIGHTED BOTTOMS TO ILLUSTRATE THEIR BELIEF THAT *BUDDHA COULD NOT FALL*

BILL BRONTHON of PRINCETON UNIVERSITY AND **GLEN CUNNINGHAM** of KANSAS 2 RUNNERS WHOSE COMPETITIONS MADE TRACK HISTORY IN THE 30's, *BOTH SUFFERED SEVERE LEG BURNS AS YOUNGSTERS-- CUNNINGHAM SO BADLY THAT HE WAS NEVER EXPECTED TO WALK AGAIN*

FRANCIS B. SILBERG A RABBI IN MILWAUKEE, WIS., AT THE AGE OF 32 SKIPPED ROPE CONTINUOUSLY FOR *4 HOURS, 10 MINUTES -- COMPLETING 35,000 JUMPS*

HAUSA THE LANGUAGE OF 15,000,000 NATIVES OF AFRICA IS READ FROM RIGHT TO LEFT—BUT IS *WRITTEN BY TURNING THE PAGE SIDEWAYS AND WRITING FROM TOP TO BOTTOM*

JOSIP KOSOR
(1879-1961)
the Yugoslav playwright
ALWAYS CUT THE HEEL AND TOE FROM EVERY NEW PAIR OF SOCKS
HE EXPLAINED THEY WOULD WEAR OUT THERE ANYWAY

JOSEPH BAYLIS of Fords, N.J., CAN PLACE **50** PENNIES ON HIS FOREARM-- FLIP THEM INTO THE AIR, **AND CATCH ALL 50 IN HIS HAND**

THE **FATHER OF THE AMERICAN FLAG**
CAPTAIN SAMUEL CHESTER REID
(1783-1861) American naval hero
SUGGESTED THE PRESENT FORM OF THE AMERICAN FLAG - *PERMANENT RETENTION OF THE 13 STRIPES AND ADDITION OF A STAR FOR EACH NEW STATE*

52

DONALD BALDWIN DISCOVERED THE PRE-HISTORIC COPPER CULTURE BURIAL GROUNDS IN OCONTO COUNTY, WIS. DATING BACK 7,510 YEARS-- *WHEN HE WAS 13 YEARS OLD*

GIRLS ATTENDING THE RUSSIAN STATE SMOLNY INSTITUTE, IN THE EARLY 20th CENTURY, WERE KEPT IN SECLUSION FOR A PERIOD OF **7** YEARS-- *DENIED PERMISSION TO SEE EVEN THEIR OWN FAMILIES*

THE **HAT** ISSUED TO U.S. SOLDIERS IN 1870 WAS TOPPED BY A TIN OIL LAMP WHICH *ILLUMINATED THEIR WAY ON DARK NIGHTS*

LEPCHA WOMEN of Sikkim, India, WEAR THEIR HAIR *IN THE SHAPE OF A HALO*

CLARENCE E. THORPE of Riverside, Calif. CAN SIMULTANEOUSLY DRAW ONE CARTOON WITH ONE HAND AND *ANOTHER WITH HIS FOOT*

The STRANGEST QUALIFICATION TEST IN HISTORY!

EMPEROR AKBAR (1542-1602) of India

FORCED EVERY CANDIDATE FOR HIGH OFFICE TO VIE WITH HIM IN A GAME OF NIGHT POLO
—USING BALLS OF FIRE!

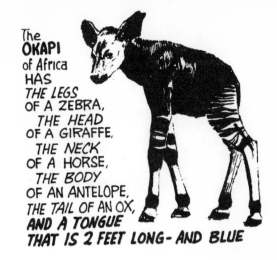

The **OKAPI** of Africa HAS *THE LEGS OF A ZEBRA, THE HEAD OF A GIRAFFE, THE NECK OF A HORSE, THE BODY OF AN ANTELOPE, THE TAIL OF AN OX, AND A TONGUE THAT IS 2 FEET LONG- AND BLUE*

BULLFIGHTS ARE STAGED REGULARLY BY THE MOROS OF JOLO, IN THE PHILIPPINE ISLANDS, BUT THE OWNERS KEEP THE BULLS ON ROPES SO THE *ANIMALS CAN ONLY SNORT AND PAW AT EACH OTHER* THE LOSER IS THE BULL THAT TIRES FIRST -AND THE VALUABLE ANIMALS ARE NEVER HARMED

"SANDY" A COLLIE HAS CHEWED 6 PACKS OF GUM EVERY DAY FOR 5 YEARS Submitted by DOROTHY ANNE SPICE, Toronto, Ont.

"BLACKIE" A FIREHOUSE DOG IN BROOKLYN SAVED A CAT FROM A BURNING BUILDING IN 1936 *BY CARRYING IT DOWN A LADDER*

KNIGHT LIGHTS KNIGHTS in medieval times WHEN ENGAGING IN BATTLES AFTER DARK *CARRIED LIGHTED LANTERNS AFFIXED TO THEIR SADDLES*

THESE HIEROGLYPHICS IN THE TIME OF THE ANCIENT PHARAOHS REPRESENTED THE FIGURE 1,235,326

Ripley's *Believe It or Not!*

A COMBINATION SOFA AND BATHTUB
was advertised in Chicago, Illinois, in 1884
AS A "HOUSEHOLD NECESSITY"

A Lincoln

RAIL S **P** LITTER
RIVE **R** MAN
DEPUTY SURV **E** YOR
PO **S** TMASTER
LEG **I** SLATOR
SOL **D** IER
GROC **E** R
ATTOR **N** EY
REPRESEN **T** ATIVE

JAMES MONROE
(1758-1831)

5th PRESIDENT OF THE UNITED STATES, WAS THE LAST U.S. PRESIDENT TO WEAR *KNEE BREECHES AND A COCKED HAT*

Tami McMURRAY
of Eureka, Calif.,
COULD WHISTLE AT THE
AGE OF 9 MONTHS

56

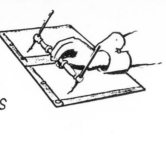

The FIRST MULTIGRAPH
PATENTED IN Cologne, Germany, in 1650 CONSISTED OF A HANDLE CONTROLLING SEVERAL PENS -WHICH COULD MAKE ONE OR MORE COPIES SIMULTANEOUSLY

A **STATUE** OF **Peter Pan** in London, England, AND AN EXACT REPLICA in Perth, Australia, WERE BOTH ERECTED IN THE DARKNESS OF A SINGLE NIGHT -TO CONVEY THE ILLUSION THAT THEY WERE THE CREATION OF FAIRIES

PRESIDENT WILLIAM HOWARD TAFT IN 1910, IN A BASEBALL GAME BETWEEN THE WASHINGTON SENATORS AND PHILADELPHIA ATHLETICS, **STARTED THE PRESIDENTIAL CUSTOM OF THROWING OUT THE FIRST BALL**

WYSTAN HUGH AUDEN (1907-1973), THE BRITISH-AMERICAN POET, MARRIED ERIKA MANN, DAUGHTER OF NOVELIST THOMAS MANN, TO ENABLE HER TO LEAVE NAZI GERMANY. THEY HAD NEVER MET PREVIOUS TO THEIR MARRIAGE, YET THEY REMAINED WEDDED UNTIL HER DEATH **33** YEARS LATER

The VIRGINIA DOUBLE CANOE COULD TRANSPORT **9 HOGSHEADS** OF TOBACCO -A TOTAL OF **4,500 POUNDS** — YET A SINGLE CANOE COULD NOT CARRY EVEN ONE HOGSHEAD

Ripley's Believe It or Not!

RINGS WERE LEGAL TENDER IN Ireland IN THE 12th CENTURY

THE ONE-STORY HOUSE WITH A SECOND FLOOR

THE ORIGINAL HERMITAGE, ANDREW JACKSON'S HOME in Nashville, Tenn., for 15 years, WAS BUILT AS A TWO-STORY CABIN, BUT WHEN THE FIRST STORY BECAME UNSAFE *THE SECOND STORY WAS LOWERED TO A POSITION ON THE GROUND*

SPINES of the Tuna Cactus of Argentina ARE USED BY THE INDIANS AS *NEEDLES*

THE FIRST MOTION PICTURE EVER MADE WAS A SOUND PICTURE!

WHEN **EDISON** DEMONSTRATED HIS LATEST INVENTION THE MOTION PICTURE, FOR THE FIRST TIME OCT. 6, 1889 — THE FILM WAS SYNCHRONIZED WITH A PHONOGRAPH WHICH EDISON HAD INVENTED 12 YRS. EARLIER

58

The **MILL** of West Ashling, England, CAN BE OPERATED BY **WATER, WIND OR STEAM**

FIRST MAN TO WIN AN ELECTION IN **AMERICA** !

REVEREND **JOHN WILSON** of Windsor, England WHO CAME OVER WITH THE FIRST BAND OF PURITANS WAS CHOSEN "PASTOR AND TEACHER" WHEN THEY LANDED AT SALEM, MASS. *THIS WAS THE FIRST BALLOT TAKEN IN THE NEW WORLD.*

The **WORKING ELEPHANTS** of Mysore, India, LABOR ONLY 4 HOURS A DAY AND ARE GUARANTEED BY LAW **3 MONTHS** *OF VACATION EACH YEAR*

2 **WILD BOARS** WERE TRAINED BY FRANCOIS BOUCHAYEZ, FAMED FRENCH SPORTSMAN, *TO SERVE AS "HUNTING DOGS"*

59

THE **TAILLESS TENREC** of Madagascar REGULARLY PRODUCES THE LARGEST LITTERS OF ANY MAMMAL - AS MANY AS **32** YOUNG AT EACH BIRTH

A **ZEBRA'S STRIPES** ARE AS INDIVIDUAL AS HUMAN FINGERPRINTS NO TWO ZEBRAS ARE STRIPED EXACTLY ALIKE

CROCODILES FOUND IN THE SHARI RIVER, AFRICA, ARE STRIPED LIKE ZEBRAS

A **RAM** ADDS AN ADDITIONAL SPIRAL SECTION TO ITS HORNS EACH YEAR

THE ELEPHANT THAT DROVE OFF A BAND OF PIRATES

"ROME" A SAILING SHIP RETURNING FROM SUMATRA WAS SAVED FROM PIRATES OFF MUSCAT, IN THE GULF OF OMAN, WHEN ITS SKIPPER, CAPTAIN SAMUEL KENNEDY, *FREED AN ELEPHANT HE WAS TRANSPORTING ON DECK*

THE SIGHT OF THE STRANGE MONSTER AND ITS TRUMPETINGS TERRIFIED THE ARAB PIRATES AND THEY FLED IN CONFUSION

THE GROUND CUCKOO
CAN RUN AS FAST AS A RACEHORSE

ALL **SIAMESE CATS** ARE BORN WHITE

CAMELS TRAVELING IN CARAVANS THROUGH THE SAHARA DESERT ARE EQUIPPED WITH HEADLIGHTS

ON NIGHT TRIPS KEROSENE LAMPS ARE SUSPENDED FROM THEIR NECKS

A **FOX** AND A **FOXHOUND** BOTH OWNED BY THE BELSTONE HUNT, ENGLAND, **BECAME GOOD FRIENDS** Submitted by Jean Reville, Brisbane, Australia

A **HIPPOPOTAMUS** CAN OPEN ITS MOUTH TO *A WIDTH OF 3 TO 4 FEET*

EDGAR ALLAN POE DID HIS BEST WRITING -WITH A CAT PERCHED ON HIS SHOULDER

61

CAMELS in the Canary Islands ARE EQUIPPED WITH RUMBLE SEATS AND TRANSPORT 2 RIDERS AND THEIR LUGGAGE

Eskimo **BABIES** in Spence Bay, Northern Canada, ARE CARRIED OUTDOORS IN FREEZING TEMPERATURES *COMPLETELY NAKED*

THE **PAPUANS** OF DOREI BAY, NEW GUINEA AS A SIGN OF MANLINESS *WEAR IN THEIR HAIR A BAMBOO COMB 2 FEET LONG AND ADORNED WITH 5 FEATHERS*

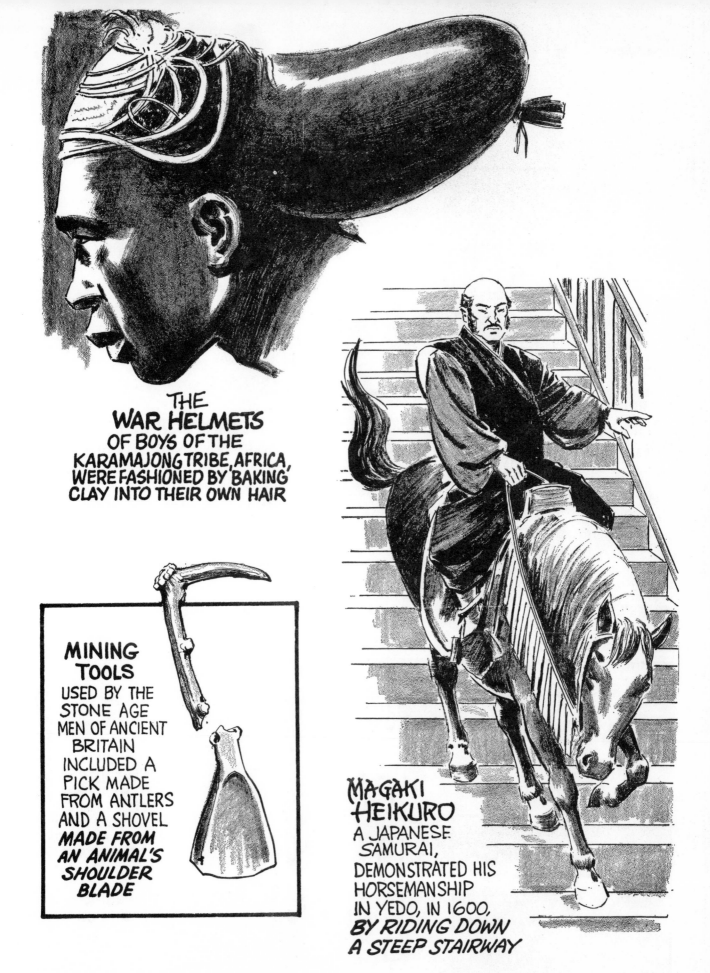

THE
WAR HELMETS
OF BOYS OF THE
KARAMAJONG TRIBE, AFRICA,
WERE FASHIONED BY 'BAKING'
CLAY INTO THEIR OWN HAIR

**MINING
TOOLS**
USED BY THE
STONE AGE
MEN OF ANCIENT
BRITAIN
INCLUDED A
PICK MADE
FROM ANTLERS
AND A SHOVEL
*MADE FROM
AN ANIMAL'S
SHOULDER
BLADE*

**MAGAKI
HEIKURO**
A JAPANESE
SAMURAI,
DEMONSTRATED HIS
HORSEMANSHIP
IN YEDO, IN 1600,
*BY RIDING DOWN
A STEEP STAIRWAY*

THE APPLE THAT MADE iBRAHIM COMMANDER OF EGYPT'S ARMY!

MOHAMMED ALI, ruler of Egypt, ANNOUNCED IN 1816 THAT HE WOULD GIVE COMMAND OF HIS ARMY TO WHOEVER COULD SECURE AN APPLE CENTERED ON A CARPET -WITHOUT SETTING FOOT ON THE CARPET

AFTER EVERY OTHER CONTESTANT HAD FAILED, IBRAHIM REACHED THE APPLE SIMPLY BY ROLLING UP THE CARPET

THE **STEEL INTERIOR SKELETON** OF THE STATUE OF LIBERTY WAS DESIGNED BY ALEXANDRE GUSTAVE EIFFEL *WHO BUILT THE EIFFEL TOWER IN PARIS, FRANCE*

A PORTABLE **DRESSING TENT** ADVERTISED IN LONDON, ENGLAND, IN THE 1920's, WAS SUPPORTED BY A TOP SHAPED LIKE A LAMP-SHADE *THAT RESTED ON THE BATHER'S HEAD*

THE **WORLD'S BIGGEST HEARING AID** CREATED IN 1819 FOR KING JOHN VI of Portugal *WAS AN ACOUSTIC-THRONE CHAIR...* COURTIERS KNELT AND SPOKE INTO THE LIONS' MOUTHS IN THE CHAIR'S HOLLOW ARMS

A **SINGLE DROP OF WATER** CONTAINS **100 BILLION, BILLION ATOMS**

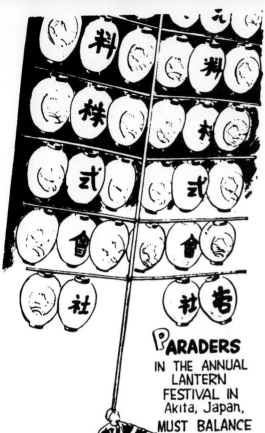

PARADERS
IN THE ANNUAL
LANTERN
FESTIVAL IN
Akita, Japan,

MUST BALANCE
ON THEIR
CHINS OR
FOREHEADS

*DOZENS OF
LANTERNS
DANGLING
FROM POLES
40 FEET
HIGH*

POST **W**INDMILLS, USED IN COLONIAL AMERICA,
WERE MOUNTED ON A POST THAT SERVED AS A TURNTABLE SO
THEIR SAILS COULD BE FACED INTO THE PREVAILING WIND

A **SQUARE
BLOCK OF
PALM LEAVES**
TIED
TOGETHER
WITH A
BRAIDED
RIBBON

*SERVES THE LOMA TRIBE of Africa
AS A FOOTBALL*

TRAVEL TRUNKS
IN COLONIAL AMERICA,
OFTEN WERE CARVED FROM
THE TRUNK OF A TREE

BATHTUB
IN JOHN PAUL JONES'
HOUSE in Portsmouth, N.H.,
HEWN FROM A MAHOGANY LOG

OTOMI
INDIANS
of Puebla,
Mexico,

ARE
CURED OF
VERTIGO BY
CLIMBING
TO THE
TOP OF A
HUGE POLE
DURING
FEAST
DAYS AND
PERFORMING
A RITUAL
DANCE

90 *FEET
IN THE
AIR*

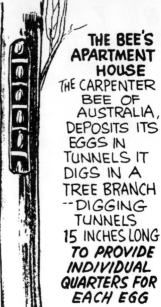

THE BEE'S APARTMENT HOUSE
THE CARPENTER BEE OF AUSTRALIA, DEPOSITS ITS EGGS IN TUNNELS IT DIGS IN A TREE BRANCH -- DIGGING TUNNELS 15 INCHES LONG *TO PROVIDE INDIVIDUAL QUARTERS FOR EACH EGG*

WILLIAM WILLIS
SAILED 6,700 MILES FROM PERU TO SAMOA IN 112 DAYS ON A RAFT CONSISTING OF 7 BALSA LOGS LASHED TOGETHER *AT THE AGE OF 61*
HIS ONLY COMPANIONS WERE A CAT AND A PARROT— *AND THE CAT ATE THE PARROT* (1954)

A CABIN
BUILT OF ROCKS near Las Vegas, Nev., IN 1869 WAS WRECKED BY A STORM THAT SAME YEAR - AND THE ROCKS WERE FOUND TO CONTAIN ORE WORTH $75,000

The STEEL MINISKIRT
KING HENRY VIII of England OFTEN WORE A COAT OF ARMS *WITH A PLEATED MINISKIRT*
THE SKIRT LOOKED LIKE CLOTH AND WAS EQUIPPED WITH HINGES SO IT COULD BE RAISED STILL HIGHER WHEN THE MONARCH WAS ON HORSEBACK

A **CHURCH**
4½ FEET HIGH,
4½ FEET LONG
AND 3 FEET WIDE,
BUILT WITH
150,000 MATCHES
Created by
MIGUEL ANGEL PRESSENDA
Parana, Argentina

A **TIN TUB**
SERVES ON THE EUPHRATES
RIVER, in Syria,
AS AN EXCURSION BOAT

A **CUP**
OF BOILING WATER
EXPOSED TO A
TEMPERATURE OF 80°
BELOW ZERO IN THE
ARCTIC INSTANTLY
TURNED INTO ICE
AND BURST WITH
A REPORT LIKE AN
EXPLOSION

T**HE INSTITUTE OF NATURAL SCIENCE**
IN DOBERAN, GERMANY,
WAS CONSTRUCTED ENTIRELY BY
20 TEACHERS AND 300 STUDENTS
--*FROM 120,000 BRICKS MADE BY*
THE STUDENTS THEMSELVES

YOUNG
GIRLS
in Nazare,
Portugal,
ARE NEVER
WELL DRESSED
WITHOUT
AT LEAST
7
PETTICOATS

THE **STRANGEST DRAMATIC SCHOOL IN HISTORY**
CHARLES DULLIN (1885-1949)
the brilliant French actor
RECEIVED HIS DRAMATIC TRAINING
RECITING POETRY DAILY FOR SEVERAL YEARS
IN A CAGE FULL OF LIONS

THE FISH WITH RUNNING LIGHTS
PHOTOSTOMIAS GUERNI IS EQUIPPED WITH 2 ROWS OF PHOSPHORESCENT SPOTS *TO LIGHT ITS WAY THROUGH THE DEPTHS OF THE OCEAN*

CHINESE PEASANTS
JOURNEYING TO MARKET, USED TO WALK SEVERAL DAYS CARRYING A 150-LB. PIG ON THEIR BACKS --SO IT WOULD NOT LOSE WEIGHT ON THE TRIP

SLEIGH DOGS in Labrador ARE TURNED LOOSE IN SUMMER AND *FEED THEMSELVES BY FISHING IN SHALLOW WATERS FOR SCULPIN AND FROG FISH*

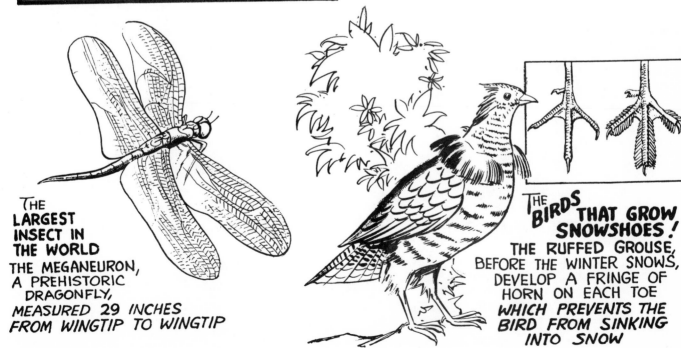

THE **LARGEST INSECT IN THE WORLD** THE MEGANEURON, A PREHISTORIC DRAGONFLY, *MEASURED 29 INCHES FROM WINGTIP TO WINGTIP*

THE **BIRDS THAT GROW SNOWSHOES!** THE RUFFED GROUSE, BEFORE THE WINTER SNOWS, DEVELOP A FRINGE OF HORN ON EACH TOE *WHICH PREVENTS THE BIRD FROM SINKING INTO SNOW*

ESKIMOS
LONG GUARDED THEMSELVES
AGAINST SNOW BLINDNESS
*BY WEARING WOODEN
GOGGLES THAT HAD
NARROW EYESLITS*

Alfred VAIL
(1807-1859) of Morristown, N.J.
INVENTED THE
ALPHABET OF
DOTS AND DASHES
*KNOWN AS THE
MORSE CODE*

SOME CHILDREN IN TAHITI
--EVEN THOSE IN PROSPEROUS
FAMILIES --*ARE NOT RAISED
BY THEIR OWN PARENTS.*
MANY FAMILIES BELIEVE IT
IS BETTER FOR CHILDREN TO
BE REARED BY STRANGERS,
WHO WILL NOT SPOIL THEM

DOROTHEA DIX
AS SUPERINTENDENT OF NURSES
IN THE CIVIL WAR,
REFUSED TO EMPLOY ANY NURSE
WHO WAS NOT HOMELY

JAMES KNOX POLK

THE 11th PRESIDENT OF THE UNITED STATES, HAD A UNIQUE RECORD OF FULFILLING EVERY PLEDGE MADE IN HIS CAMPAIGN-- *YET HE WAS THE FIRST PRESIDENT TO REFUSE TO RUN FOR REELECTION.*

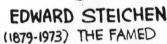

EDWARD STEICHEN

(1879-1973) THE FAMED PHOTOGRAPHER, SEEKING A PERFECT PRINT, ONCE SPENT A FULL YEAR, AND TOOK 1,000 PHOTOS OF A WHITE CUP AND SAUCER

A KITE

ENTERED IN A CONTEST IN HAMDEN, CONN., FLEW AT A HEIGHT OF 100 FEET FOR TWO HOURS ALTHOUGH IT MEASURED ONLY *6" BY 2" BY 2"*

Designed and submitted by Harry N. Gambardella New Haven, Conn.

EMILY DICKINSON (1830-1886)

THE POET -- CONSIDERED HERSELF SO UGLY, THAT WHEN CONVERSING WITH A VISITOR IN HER HOME, *SHE ALWAYS REMAINED IN ANOTHER ROOM, TALKING THROUGH AN OPEN DOOR*

1st EARL OF CRAWFORD

(1365-1407) DURING A TOURNAMENT ON LONDON BRIDGE, ENGLAND, LEAPED OFF HIS HORSE AND MOUNTED IT AGAIN-- *WHILE WEARING A FULL SUIT OF ARMOR (MAY 6, 1390)*

THE SHIPWRECKED SAILORS WHO WERE SAVED BY A SPRING −1,500 MILES AT SEA!

THE CREW OF THE SAILING SHIP "LARA", DRIFTING IN 3 LIFEBOATS IN THE PACIFIC OCEAN WEST OF THE COAST OF MEXICO, AFTER THE VESSEL HAD BEEN DESTROYED BY FIRE, WAS SAVED WHEN THE CAPTAIN NOTICED THAT THE WATER HAD CHANGED FROM BLUE TO GREEN −AND FOUND THAT THE BOATS WERE OVER A FRESH-WATER SPRING

7 OF THE CREWMEN WERE UNCONSCIOUS FROM THIRST, BUT ALL SURVIVED AND THE CREW FINALLY REACHED MEXICO 23 DAYS AFTER THE SHIPWRECK   (1881)

BOAT TRIPS ARE OFTEN MADE IN THE ARCTIC OVER THE ICE − THE MIDNIGHT SUN MELTS THE SNOW ATOP THE ETERNAL ICE AND PEOPLE PADDLE IN THE SWEET-WATER LAKE FORMED BY THE THAW

SPINES of the SEA URCHIN, WHICH ARE ABOUT 6 INCHES LONG, ARE USED BY SCHOOL-CHILDREN OF RAROTONGA, IN THE PACIFIC, AS SLATE PENCILS

THE FIRST WAR MEMORIAL BUILT WITH ENEMY ARMOR
THE COLOSSUS of RHODES

ONE OF THE SEVEN WONDERS OF THE ANCIENT WORLD - A COPPER STATUE THAT TOWERED **107** FEET ABOVE THE ISLAND OF RHODES—WAS CONSTRUCTED *FROM THE WAR MACHINES ABANDONED BY A SYRIAN ARMY THAT HAD TRIED IN VAIN TO BATTER DOWN THE ISLAND'S FORTIFICATIONS FOR AN ENTIRE YEAR*

(304 B.C.)

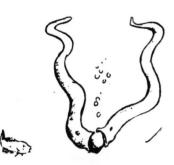

LAMPREY EELS
CONSTRUCT NESTS 3 FT. HIGH AND 4 FT. IN DIAMETER ON THE SEA BOTTOM--*BOTH PARENTS LABORING TOGETHER TO CARRY HEAVY STONES*

THE **REDSHANK**
AFTER ITS YOUNG HAVE HATCHED PICKS UP EVERY PIECE OF EGG SHELL FROM THE GROUND SO ITS ENEMIES WILL NOT HAVE A CLUE TO THE LOCATION OF ITS NEST

THE **TUNA** IS THE ONLY FISH WITH A BLOOD TEMPERATURE **HIGHER THAN THE WATER IN WHICH IT SWIMS**

A **SNAIL**
CAN PULL 60 TIMES ITS OWN WEIGHT -AND LIFT 10 TIMES ITS WEIGHT- A MAN WITH COMPARABLE STRENGTH COULD PULL 4 TONS AND LIFT 3/4 OF A TON

THE **GOLDEN TREE FROG**
HAS A CROAK IN WINTER THAT SOUNDS LIKE A MALLET CHIPPING ROCK *BUT IN SUMMER IT SOUNDS LIKE A TINKLING BELL*

THE **NEWARS** of Katmandu, Nepal, CARRY THEIR CHILDREN IN BASKETS *SLUNG FROM A SHOULDER YOKE*

NIGERIAN CHILDREN
WHO SUFFER FROM A HEADACHE DON A HAT TOPPED BY CARVED FIGURES *DEPICTING A DOCTOR ON HIS WAY TO VISIT A PATIENT* A PHYSICIAN'S POWERS ARE CONSIDERED SO MIRACULOUS THAT EVEN THIS CARVING WILL CURE THE HEADACHE

CHILDREN of Penrhyn Island in the Pacific, PADDLE TO SCHOOL EVERY DAY IN *WOODEN BATHTUBS*

GIANT SHEATHS
THAT PROTECT THE BUDS ON PALM TREES, ARE USED BY NATIVES IN THE BRAZILIAN JUNGLE *AS BATHTUBS*

INFANTS
IN THE TORTOISE TOTEM OF THE OSAGE INDIANS WERE GIVEN HAIRCUTS INDICATING *THE HEAD, PAWS AND TAIL OF A TORTOISE*

CHARLES BEVERUNG
DRUMMER BOY ON THE SHIP "LADY ELGIN" WHICH SANK WITH A LOSS OF 297 LIVES IN LAKE MICHIGAN *SAVED HIMSELF BY SWIMMING TO SHORE - USING HIS DRUM AS A LIFE PRESERVER !*
(Sept. 8, 1860)

SCHOOLCHILDREN
of Ravensburg, Germany, ANNUALLY MARCH SWINGING LONG SWITCHES -TO COMMEMORATE THE 14th CENTURY PLAGUE WHEN EVERYONE WAS SO AFRAID OF CATCHING THE DISEASE **THEY WAVED LONG TWIGS AT EACH OTHER INSTEAD OF SHAKING HANDS**

DOLLS USED IN COLONIAL AMERICA *WERE OFTEN MADE OF TIN*

A STEEP STAIRWAY
ON ST. HELENA ISLAND, WHERE NAPOLEON I DIED, HAS 699 STEPS AND A LENGTH OF 933 FEET -YET NATIVE BOYS GO UP AND DOWN IT IN LESS THAN 8 MINUTES- THEY HAVE LEARNED TO DESCEND BY SLIDING DOWN THE RAILINGS -LYING WITH THEIR HEAD ON ONE RAIL AND THEIR FEET OVER THE OTHER

A 2-WHEELED CART
WAS ADVERTISED IN LEEDS, ENGLAND, IN THE 1800s "FOR DEVELOPING THE PHYSIQUE" OF YOUNG BOYS AND GIRLS FROM THE AGE OF 4 TO 12

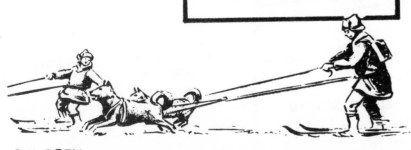

CHILDREN
of the Nanay Tribe, Siberia, TRAVEL TO AND FROM THEIR DISTANT SCHOOL ON SKIS---**PULLED BY DOGS**

Ripley's Believe It or Not!

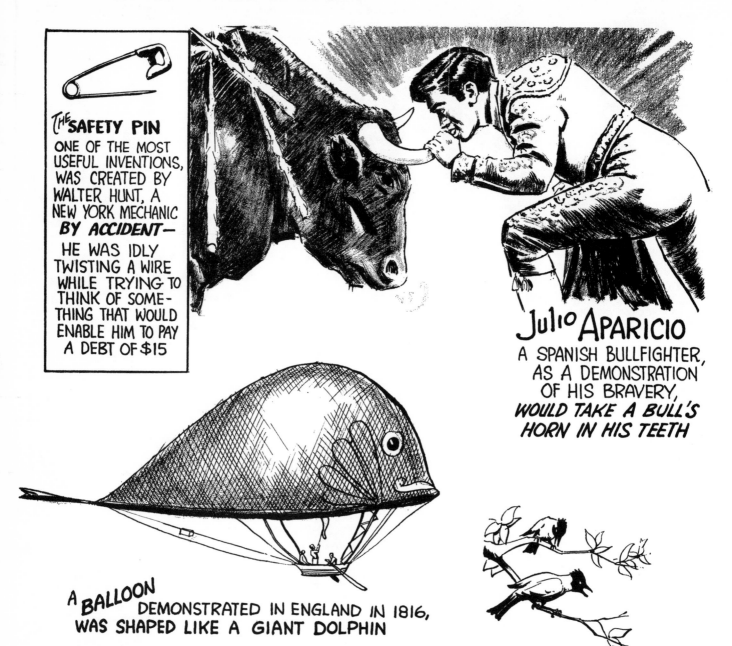

THE SAFETY PIN

ONE OF THE MOST USEFUL INVENTIONS, WAS CREATED BY WALTER HUNT, A NEW YORK MECHANIC **BY ACCIDENT—**

HE WAS IDLY TWISTING A WIRE WHILE TRYING TO THINK OF SOMETHING THAT WOULD ENABLE HIM TO PAY A DEBT OF $15

Julio APARICIO

A SPANISH BULLFIGHTER, AS A DEMONSTRATION OF HIS BRAVERY, *WOULD TAKE A BULL'S HORN IN HIS TEETH*

A **BALLOON** DEMONSTRATED IN ENGLAND IN 1816, WAS SHAPED LIKE A GIANT DOLPHIN

THE TOPPIE
an African bird

BY SETTING UP AN INCESSANT CHATTER ALWAYS WARNS PASSERSBY OF THE PRESENCE OF *A CONCEALED SNAKE*

THE "WHITE SUGAR" SANDS OF ALAMOGORDO
THE ROLLING DUNES OF THE DESERT WEST OF ALAMOGORDO, NEW MEXICO, COVERING SOME 270 SQ. MILES, LOOK LIKE *MOUNDS OF GRANULATED SUGAR*

LAPP SKIERS

OFTEN LEAP CHASMS **125 FEET** WIDE

THE **LARGEST DRUMS IN THE WORLD**
THE **NAGAS** of Assam, India, COVER HOLLOWED-OUT TREE TRUNKS WITH SKIN TO BUILD DRUMS SO LARGE EACH CAN BE BEATEN BY **50 DRUMMERS SIMULTANEOUSLY**

THE **KHMER KINGS** of Cambodia, IN ANCIENT TIMES WERE TRANSPORTED IN 2-WHEELED CARTS OF GOLD - PULLED BY SERVANTS WHO WORE HEADDRESSES IN THE SHAPE OF HORSES' HEADS

THEODORE ROOSEVELT
SHOT IN THE RIGHT LUNG BY A FANATIC DURING HIS 1912 CAMPAIGN FOR THE PRESIDENCY, MADE A CAMPAIGN SPEECH AS SCHEDULED A FEW HOURS LATER, SAYING: *"THERE IS A BULLET IN MY BODY, BUT IT TAKES MORE THAN THAT TO KILL A BULL MOOSE."*

MARK TWAIN MADE A FORTUNE AS A WRITER, BUT LOST IT ALL AS AN UNSUCCESSFUL **INVENTOR**

AMERICA'S SMALLEST PRESIDENT
James Madison
THE 4th PRESIDENT OF THE UNITED STATES *WAS UNDER 5'6" TALL AND WEIGHED BUT 100 LBS.*

TEDDY ROOSEVELT
EVEN DURING THE PERIODS HE SERVED AS PRESIDENT OF THE UNITED STATES AND AS VICE PRESIDENT AND AS GOVERNOR OF NEW YORK, STILL FOUND TIME **TO READ 2 OR 3 BOOKS A DAY**

Amelia Jenks BLOOMER (1818-1894), THE FEMINIST, IN 1849 FOUNDED "THE LILY" --THE FIRST AMERICAN PUBLICATION EDITED BY, AND FOR, WOMEN

QUEEN ELIZABETH I OF ENGLAND, HAD 2,000 GOWNS -- WHICH WERE KEPT IN A SEPARATE *CLOTHING HOUSE*

ABRAHAM LINCOLN WAS THE ONLY PRESIDENT OF THE UNITED STATES WHO WHILE SERVING AS COMMANDER-IN-CHIEF *ACTUALLY WITNESSED A BATTLE AND WAS EXPOSED TO ENEMY FIRE* Fort Stevens, Washington, D.C., June 11, 1864

CAPT. WILLIAM KIDD (1645-1701), BEFORE HE BECAME AN INFAMOUS PIRATE, *WAS RESPECTED AS A TRADER ON NEW YORK'S WALL STREET*

THE PELICAN EEL
FOUND AT A DEPTH OF ONE MILE IN THE BERMUDA SEAS, HAS A RED TAIL THAT IS **3 TIMES AS LONG AS ITS BLACK BODY**

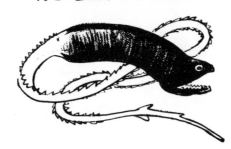

NATURE'S FLOWER CHILDREN
EACH PINK FLOWER OF THE PURPLE ORCHID LOOKS REMARKABLY LIKE A SMALL CHILD WEARING A HAT TOO LARGE FOR IT

THE COCONUT CRAB
OF THE INDIAN AND PACIFIC OCEANS, WHICH IS **3 FEET** LONG AND WEIGHS **6 POUNDS,** CLIMBS TREES, HURLS COCONUTS TO THE GROUND **AND CAN OPEN CRACKED ONES WITH ITS POWERFUL CLAWS**

THE **"OSTRICH" BEETLE**
THE DARKLING BEETLE, WHEN THREATENED, **STANDS ON ITS HEAD**

THE COCKROACH
IS THE OLDEST OF ALL INSECTS -- *HAVING SURVIVED UNCHANGED FOR OVER 100,000,000 YEARS*

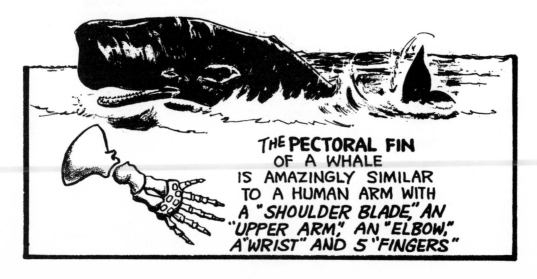

THE **PECTORAL FIN**
OF A WHALE IS AMAZINGLY SIMILAR TO A HUMAN ARM WITH A "SHOULDER BLADE," AN "UPPER ARM," AN "ELBOW," A "WRIST" AND 5 "FINGERS"

THE **MUDSKIPPER** BREATHES WHILE ON LAND *THROUGH THE TAIL WHICH IT KEEPS DIPPED IN THE WATER*

THE **SAW-WHET OWL** IS SO NAMED BECAUSE ITS HOOT *SOUNDS LIKE THE HONING OF A SAW*

ANT NESTS IN THE LOCHA FOREST OF AFRICA, ARE SO BUFFETED BY RAIN THAT THEIR OCCUPANTS BUILD A NEW ROOF EACH SEASON *-ERECTING EACH ROOF ATOP THE OLD ONE !*

TERMITE NESTS IN AFRICA PROJECT ABOVE GROUND *HUGE SHAFTS TO SUPPLY FRESH AIR*

THE **FLYING GURNARD** SWIMS IN WATER, WALKS ON LAND, AND FLIES THROUGH THE AIR

THE **BRAZILIAN COELOXENUS BEETLE** IS SUPPORTED AS A GUEST IN ANTS' NESTS BECAUSE ITS WINGS ARE COVERED WITH LONG HAIRS *EACH OF WHICH EXUDES HONEY*

A HOUSE DIVIDED

A HOME BUILT IN ZEYERN, IN NO. BAVARIA, BY BROTHERS KARL AND HANNES REBHUHN--*WHO COULDN'T AGREE ON ITS DESIGN*

Submitted by Emery F. Tobin, Vancouver, Wash.

POLE VAULTING
FOR DISTANCE RATHER THAN HEIGHT IS A SPORT ONLY IN THE NETHERLANDS --*WHERE IT IS ALSO A MEANS OF CROSSING UNBRIDGED CANALS*-- GERRIT VALKEMA, OF JOURE, HOLDS THE RECORD WITH A VAULT OF *41 FEET, 8½ INCHES*

CAVERN APARTMENT HOUSE
A COLONY OF CAVE DWELLERS IN Tripoli, Libya, OCCUPIES A 4-STORY DWELLING IN A CAVE *50 FEET HIGH*

THE GREAT DITCH
SURROUNDING THE WADDEN ISLANDS In The Netherlands FOR YEARS HAD TO BE CROSSED PART WAY BY RAFT PART WAY BY BOAT *AND THEN IN A WHEELED HORSE-DRAWN CART*

WILLIAM R. SANDFORD
(1868-1950) of Margaretville, N.Y.,
A ONE-ARMED TRUCK DRIVER, RODE HIS VEHICLE DOWN A **50**-FOOT EMBANKMENT TO A RAILROAD TRACK AND THEN CAREENED INTO THE DELAWARE RIVER *-YET EMERGED UNHURT*

COCONUT TREES ARE PROTECTED FROM THIEVES IN THE SOLOMON ISLANDS BY A *SYMBOLIC LIKENESS OF A CROCODILE*

PITTOST, A PROFESSIONAL SMUGGLER OF CARNIA, ITALY, ELUDED CUSTOMS GUARDS ON HIS JOURNEYS ACROSS THE BORDER BY WEARING BOOTS ON WHICH THE *HEELS AND SOLES WERE REVERSED*

THE DOG THAT SAVED 92 LIVES!

THE S.S. ETHIE, A COASTAL STEAMER OF 414 TONS, AGROUND ON MARTIN'S POINT OFF CURLING, NEWFOUNDLAND, AND BREAKING UP IN A VIOLENT STORM AND HEAVY SEAS, WAS UNABLE TO FIRE A LIFELINE OR LAUNCH ITS BOATS, AND *NO MEMBER OF THE CREW DARED ATTEMPT TO SWIM ASHORE*

A NEWFOUNDLAND DOG MADE THE SWIM WITH A LIFELINE GRIPPED IN ITS TEETH AND ALL 92 PASSENGERS AND CREW MEMBERS WERE PULLED TO SAFETY ON A BOATSWAIN'S CHAIR (Dec. 10, 1919)

WOLF ROCK LIGHTHOUSE

OFF THE COAST OF Cornwall, England, CUT OFF FROM SUPPLIES BY ROUGH SEAS FOR 25 DAYS, WAS DELIVERED FOOD FROM A STORM-TOSSED SHIP *BY MEANS OF A KITE MADE FROM AN OLD FLOUR BAG*
(1952)

The **BRIDGE OF TREES** near Ourakana Totiong, Sudan, Africa— TREES GROWING IN THE BED OF A RIVER 50 FEET WIDE HAVE BECOME SO ENTWINED *THAT THEIR BRANCHES SERVE NATIVES AS A BRIDGE*

THE **LAUTER RIVER** In Lauterbach, Germany, HAS A MODERN BRIDGE, BUT PEDESTRIANS STILL CROSS THE RIVER ON *ITS ANCIENT STEPPING STONES*

The **LARGEST** SHIP MODEL IN THE WORLD **THE LAGODA,** A HALF-SIZE REPLICA OF AN ACTUAL WHALING SHIP IN THE WHALING MUSEUM, NEW BEDFORD, MASS., *IS 59 FEET LONG AND HAS A MAST 50 FEET HIGH*

THE HUMAN BRIDGES

JAPANESE TROOPS INVADING MALAYA IN WORLD WAR II CROSSED SWAMPS AND SHALLOW BODIES OF WATER ON BRIDGES CONSISTING OF LOGS *SUPPORTED ON THE SHOULDERS OF SPECIALLY TRAINED ENGINEERS*

THE **TOMB** OF MOHAMMED ASKIA, RULER OF GAO, West Africa, WAS BUILT DURING HIS LIFETIME FROM A VERBAL DESCRIPTION OF THE PYRAMIDS OF EGYPT

BEFORE HIS DEATH THE KING VISITED EGYPT IN 1493 AND DISCOVERED HIS TOMB WAS NOTHING LIKE THE PYRAMIDS-BUT HE LIKED HIS IMPERFECT COPY BETTER THAN THE ORIGINAL

A **CATERPILLAR** HAS NEARLY 4 TIMES AS MANY MUSCLES **AS A MAN** - *THE CATERPILLAR HAS 2,000, A MAN 510*

W U. O.

A **REBUS** USED IN THE U.S. 100 YEARS AGO TO DUN DEBTORS— IT READS: FORK OVER W-HAT YOU OWE

A **BEANPOD** (Entada Pursoetha) in Eastern Pakistan, GROWS TO A HEIGHT OF 4 FEET AND IS SO STURDY THAT THE ARAKANESE USE IT AS A STAIRWAY TO THEIR DWELLINGS

BAN THE BOW AND ARROW

GEESE WERE RAISED BY THE ANCIENT GREEKS NOT FOR FOOD - *BUT TO PROVIDE FEATHERS FOR ARROWS*

THE **BLADDERWORT** an aquatic plant that floats in ponds, HAS TRAP DOORS IN ITS LEAVES THROUGH WHICH MINUTE WATER ORGANISMS ENTER *-BUT CAN NEVER LEAVE-* THE DEAD BODIES OF THE ORGANISMS HELP KEEP THE PLANT AFLOAT

A **DEAD SHARK** SINKS SO SLOWLY THAT ITS BODY IS ALMOST COMPLETELY DISSOLVED BY THE SALT WATER BEFORE IT REACHES THE BOTTOM OF THE SEA — THE ONLY PART OF THE SHARK THAT IS IMPERVIOUS TO THE ACTION OF THE SALT IS ITS TEETH

THE FIRST FLYING SAUCER

A RING-SHAPED MONOPLANE FLOWN BY TILGHMAN RICHARDS AND CEDRIC LEE OF ENGLAND, *IN 1914*

AN **AUSTRALIAN FROG** (Cheiroleptes Platycephalus) AWARE THAT A DROUGHT IS PENDING FILLS UP WITH WATER UNTIL IT SWELLS LIKE A BALLOON - THEN SLEEPS FOR AS LONG AS 18 MONTHS

THE MOST EXPERT SPEAR THROWERS IN THE WORLD

THE MANDAN INDIANS of North Dakota REGULARLY PLAYED A GAME *IN WHICH A LONG SPEAR WAS HURLED THROUGH A SMALL WOODEN RING AS IT ROLLED PAST ON THE GROUND*

THE **CATERPILLAR** of the Lycaenida butterfly **ALWAYS FORMS A PARTNERSHIP WITH AN ANT**

THE CATERPILLAR RELEASES A SUGARY LIQUID WHICH FEEDS THE ANT - AND THE ANT PRODUCES A HONEY THAT IS EATEN BY THE CATERPILLAR

CHILDREN of the Anyuau Tribe of Ethiopia, WHEN SWIMMING IN THE BARO RIVER, ALWAYS JOIN HANDS TO FORM A "V," SPLASH AND SHOUT - *IN THE BELIEF THAT BY IMPERSONATING A SEA MONSTER THEY WILL FRIGHTEN AWAY CROCODILES*

"MOUCHE" A POODLE OWNED BY THE LAYARD FAMILY of Florence, Italy, WAS SO TERRIFIED OF THE DARK THAT HE WOULD NOT LEAVE THE HOUSE AT NIGHT UNLESS A LIGHTED LANTERN WAS HUNG FROM HIS NECK

THE HUMAN CORK!
CASIMIR POLEMUS of Ploërmel, France,
WAS INVOLVED IN 3 SHIPWRECKS
- AND *EACH TIME WAS THE SOLE SURVIVOR!*
HE WAS THE SOLE SURVIVOR OF THE "JEANNE
CATHERINE," WRECKED OFF BREST ON JULY 11, 1875,
THE "TROIS FRÈRES," WRECKED IN THE BAY OF
BISCAY ON SEPT. 4, 1880, AND "L'ODEON," WRECKED
OFF NEWFOUNDLAND ON JAN. 1, 1882

A **BIRD REFUGE** near Stonewall, Manitoba, HAS A 400-YARD POND *IN THE SHAPE OF A DUCK* Submitted by PAM DE WEESE, Long Beach, New York

LEONARDO da VINCI (1452-1519) FAMED PAINTER, SCULPTOR, DESIGNER AND ARCHITECT, *WAS ALSO ONE OF HISTORY'S FIRST ALPINISTS.* AT THE AGE OF **59** HE CLIMBED MT. BO (8,410')

THE CAT THAT MADE A WILL **MARGUERITE MATTIGNON** of Paris, France, A 17th CENTURY HEIRESS HAD TURNED OVER A LARGE FORTUNE TO HER CAT – SO AT THE ADVICE OF HER ATTORNEYS *SHE PREPARED A RECIPROCAL WILL WHICH MADE HER THE PET'S HEIRESS* **THE CAT SIGNED THE DOCUMENT WITH AN INKED PAW**

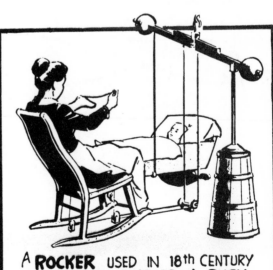

A **ROCKER** USED IN 18th CENTURY NEW ENGLAND ENABLED A BUSY MOTHER TO ROCK THE BABY'S CRADLE, CHURN THE BUTTER *–AND STILL HAVE BOTH HANDS FREE TO DARN SOCKS*

BLACK WATER BUFFALOES ARE ALWAYS BORN WHITE

THE LARGEST EGG *IS THAT OF A SHARK -* IT AVERAGES 8 7/10 INCHES IN DIAMETER

THE SPADE FISH CAN CHANGE ITS COLOR INSTANTANEOUSLY AND APPEAR BLACK, WHITE OR *BLACK AND WHITE*

ORGANPIPE CORAL GROWS IN THE SHAPE OF CYLINDRICAL TUBES *-LIKE THE PIPES OF AN ORGAN*

THE **CHINESE TUMBLER GOLDFISH** CANNOT SWIM NORMALLY - ITS ONLY MEANS OF MOVEMENT BEING A SERIES OF BACKWARD SOMERSAULTS

THE **HIPPOPOTAMUS** *WHILE IN THE WATER* OFTEN IS CLEANED OF ALGAE AND DEAD SKIN *BY A NUMBER OF CARP-LIKE FISH THAT CLING TO THE HIPPO'S SKIN BY MEANS OF SUCKERS*

9½-INCH BROOK TROUT
CAUGHT INSIDE THE
**CENTER HOLE OF A 45 RPM
PHONOGRAPH RECORD**
WAS HOOKED BY
BOBBY CUNNINGHAM
of Belfast, Me.

A WHALE
HARPOONED OFF THE COAST OF
AUSTRALIA, WAS CAPTURED BY THE
WHALER "JOHN and WINTHROP"
*ONLY AFTER IT HAD BITTEN IN
HALF 2 WHALEBOATS (1886)*

CROCODILE HUNTERS in Papua
CAPTURE THE FEROCIOUS MONSTERS
BY DIVING BENEATH THEM AND
TICKLING THEIR STOMACHS

THE SAND
on the shore of the Red Sea
on the Sinai Peninsula
*IS COMPOSED ENTIRELY OF THE
SHELLS OF PENEROPLIS*
IT IS THE ONLY PLACE ON EARTH
WHERE THE SAND CONSISTS OF
THE SHELLS OF THESE ORGANISMS

**THE FISH THAT CARRIES
A FLASHLIGHT**
GIGANTACTIS, WHICH SWIMS AT A DEPTH OF 6,000 FEET, LIGHTS
IT'S WAY THROUGH THE OCEAN DEPTHS BY A BRIGHT LIGHT IT
CARRIES AT THE END OF A ROD PROJECTING FROM ITS HEAD

THE MOST STRENUOUS RACE IN HISTORY

GIPSY MOTH III, A YACHT WEIGHING 13 TONS, AND 39 FEET, 7 INCHES LONG, WHICH NORMALLY REQUIRES A CREW OF 6 MEN, WON A RACE FROM PLYMOUTH, ENGLAND, TO NEW YORK WITH ONLY FRANCIS CHARLES CHICHESTER, AGED 59, ABOARD— CHICHESTER, RACING FOUR OTHER YACHTS EACH MANNED BY A SINGLE SAILOR, COVERED 4,000 MILES IN 40½ DAYS (June 11 TO July 21, 1960)

"ROLLIE" a PENGUIN IN THE SAN DIEGO, CALIF., ZOO, IS SO SKILLED ON ROLLER SKATES THAT HE WAS MADE *AN OFFICIAL MEMBER OF THE ROLLER SKATING ASSOCIATION*

"Cricket" A CHIHUAHUA OWNED BY MRS. LEOTA WOOSELY OF LA PUENTE, CALIF., HAS ON HER BACK THE MARKINGS OF *A CLOWN'S FACE*

A **TREE HOUSE** ON A FARM near Savigliano, Italy, CONSTRUCTED BY SHAPING AND CUTTING *THE LEAVES AND BRANCHES OF A HUGE MAPLE TREE*

TRICYCLE **10** FEET HIGH MADE BY JAMES P. GLASS OF RIVERSIDE, CALIF., *TO RIDE IN PARADES*

CAN YOU FIND THE FOUR ARROWS? *SOLUTION:*

93

THE PINE TREE SHILLING

A SILVER COIN ISSUED BY THE FIRST COLONIAL MINT, WAS REISSUED FOR A PERIOD OF 30 YEARS-- BUT THE 1652 DATE WAS NEVER CHANGED

THE FIRST AMERICAN LIE DETECTOR—MANUEL BORONDA

A RANCHER OF THE Salinas Valley, Calif., CONCEIVED IN 1840 THE IDEA OF ORDERING A SUSPECTED THIEF TO HOLD ONE OF HIS FINGERS IN A PAN CONTAINING 2 INCHES OF WATER

IF THE SUSPECT LIED AN INVOLUNTARY NERVOUS REACTION CAUSED RIPPLES IN THE WATER

THE BILLOWING BELLES OF BACSKA

FARM GIRLS in Bacska, Yugoslavia, UPON REACHING MARRIAGEABLE AGE DON **7** PETTICOATS

—AND ADD ANOTHER FOR EACH YEAR THEY REMAIN SINGLE

MARRIED WOMEN ALWAYS WEAR THE NUMBER OF PETTICOATS THEY USED AT THE TIME OF THEIR WEDDING

"HEADS I WIN— TAILS YOU LOSE"

AN AMERICAN PENNY ISSUED IN 1784 *HAD A PORTRAIT OF WASHINGTON* **ON BOTH SIDES**

THE HANGING GARDENS of VENEZUELA

INDIANS in the Orinoco forests TO PROTECT THEIR VEGETABLES FROM ANTS AND ANIMALS *PLANT THEIR CROPS IN SOIL IN CANOES ON FRAMES HIGH ABOVE THE GROUND*

STONE COLUMNS

ARE CONSTRUCTED BY PAPI NATIVES of Iran IN THEIR FIELDS AND GARDENS *BECAUSE IN THE MOONLIGHT THEY SERVE AS SCARECROWS*

LITTER BUS

WHOLE FAMILIES in old China WOULD RIDE IN A **SINGLE LITTER**— LITTERS ACCOMMODATING AS MANY AS A DOZEN PERSONS WERE IN USE UNTIL 1914

THE BRONZE "PURSE"

A RING FROM WHICH DANGLES THE RING MONEY OF THE PERIOD, WAS FOUND IN A GRAVE AT WOLLISHOFEN, SWITZERLAND, WHERE IT HAD LAIN FOR *MORE THAN 2,800 YEARS*

TIGHT-ROPE WALKERS

in Jaipur, India, MUST LEARN TO WALK A HIGH ROPE *BAREFOOT AND BLINDFOLDED*

THE **WHITE PELICAN** IS KEPT AFLOAT IN THE WATER BY *A BUILT-IN PNEUMATIC LIFE PRESERVER* A LARGE POCKET UNDER ITS SKIN IS INFLATED WITH AIR DRAWN IN THROUGH OPENINGS AT THE ROOTS OF ITS FEATHERS

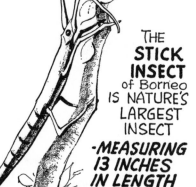

THE **STICK INSECT** of Borneo IS NATURE'S LARGEST INSECT -MEASURING 13 INCHES IN LENGTH

SIGNATURE OF C. SHARPE-MINOR AN ORGANIST of Los Angeles, Calif.

A **ROLLING CLOCK** made in France in 1680 ROLLED DOWN AN INCLINED PLANE AND WAS WOUND BY RESTORING IT TO ITS STARTING POSITION

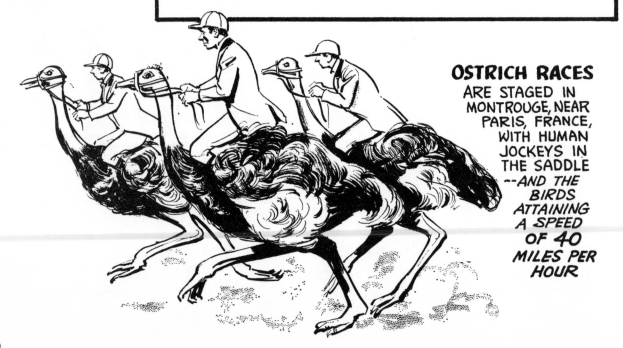

OSTRICH RACES ARE STAGED IN MONTROUGE, NEAR PARIS, FRANCE, WITH HUMAN JOCKEYS IN THE SADDLE --AND THE BIRDS ATTAINING A SPEED OF **40** MILES PER HOUR

OPTICAL ILLUSION
THE SQUARE THAT MOVES FROM ONE PRISM TO ANOTHER

Drawn by JEFFREY GOLLER, Iselin, N.J.

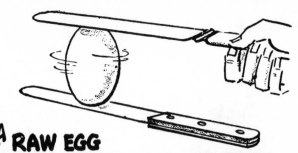

A RAW EGG
BALANCED VERTICALLY ON ITS POINTS BETWEEN THE BLADES OF **2** STEEL KNIVES
WILL ALWAYS ROTATE
Submitted by ELSA LEPPICH, Seattle, Wash.

OPTICAL ILLUSION
IS IT A PYRAMID OR A WELL?

Drawn by Thomas Heller (Age 9) Lombard, Ill.

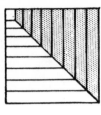

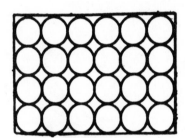

BOX CONTAINING **24** BASEBALLS

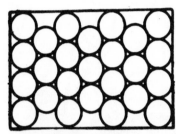

SAME BOX CONTAINING **25** BASEBALLS OF EXACTLY THE SAME SIZE

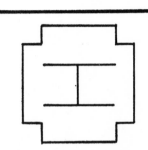

CAN YOU DIVIDE THIS PIECE OF CARDBOARD INTO 8 EQUAL SECTIONS BY UTILIZING THE 3 CUTS ALREADY IN IT?

Solution:

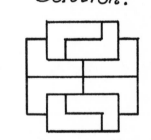

CAN YOU DRAW THIS DESIGN WITH A CONTINUOUS LINE, WITHOUT RETRACING A LINE ANYWHERE AND WITHOUT CROSSING ANY LINE?

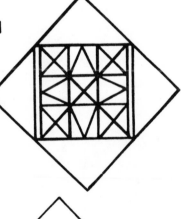

SOLUTION:
Submitted by DAVID W. TESKE New York City.

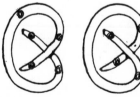

CAN YOU CUT THESE 2 PRETZEL SHAPES INTO 9 SECTIONS, EACH WITH A RAISIN EMBEDDED IN IT, WITH A SINGLE STROKE?

Solution:

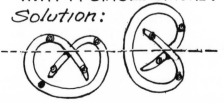

THE SHOEMAKER WHOSE LIFE WAS SAVED BY A BIRTHMARK!
IGNACIO CUEVAS, A SHOEMAKER WHO HAD BEEN SENTENCED TO THE GALLOWS
FOR A POLITICAL CRIME, WAS PARDONED BY THE COUNT DE REVILLAGIGEDO,
THE SPANISH VICEROY OF MEXICO, WHEN THE HUMBLE DEFENDANT REVEALED
HE WAS THE VICEROY'S FATHER
BY RECALLING THAT THE COUNT HAD THE MARK OF A DOVE ON HIS RIGHT ARM
THE SHOEMAKER PROVED HE HAD PLACED THE VICEROY IN AN ORPHANAGE AFTER
HIS WIFE HAD DIED IN CHILDBIRTH--LEAVING HIM WITH 16 OTHER CHILDREN
1789

BLANCHE KELSO BRUCE
WHO SERVED IN THE MISSISSIPPI STATE SENATE FROM 1875 UNTIL 1881, *WAS AN ESCAPED SLAVE*

THE **METEOR**
BUILT AT NYACK, N.Y. IN 1882, *WAS THE FIRST STEAMSHIP CONSTRUCTED WITHOUT MASTS--* FOR 100 YEARS STEAMSHIPS HAD KEPT THEIR SAILS IN CASE THE ENGINES FAILED

SHOES IN COLONIAL AMERICA COULD BE WORN **ON EITHER FOOT**

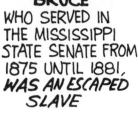

THE **NEST** OF THE LANCEOLATE HONEY EATER OF AUSTRALIA IS CONSTRUCTED AS A HAMMOCK *WHICH SWINGS FROM A BRANCH OF THE MYAL TREE*

WILLIAM LLOYD GARRISON (1805-1879) THE ABOLITIONIST, HAD TO BE JAILED FOR HIS OWN SAFETY ON OCT. 21, 1835, WHEN A MOB OF 2000 TRIED TO LYNCH HIM IN BOSTON, MASS., FOR PREACHING THAT "ALL MEN ARE CREATED EQUAL"

Ripley's Believe It or Not!

THE CHAMELEON
HAS EYES INDEPENDENT OF EACH OTHER AND CAN SIMULTANEOUSLY LOOK IN 2 DIRECTIONS

A BLUE HOMING PIGEON
TRANSPORTED FROM SAIGON, VIETNAM, TO ARRAS, FRANCE, IN THE DARK HOLD OF A SHIP, FOUND ITS WAY BACK TO SAIGON IN **25** DAYS —A JOURNEY OF **7,200** MILES WITHOUT A SINGLE FAMILIAR LANDMARK
August, 1931

THE VENUS FLOWER BASKET, A SPONGE
FOUND IN BOTH THE ATLANTIC AND PACIFIC, ACTUALLY IS A GLASS CORNUCOPIA WITH AN EXQUISITE PATTERN OF SAND SPIKES--SO BEAUTIFUL THAT NATIVES OF SOUTHERN ASIA *WEAR IT AS JEWELRY.*

THE SPONGE CRAB
TO MAKE ITSELF UNAPPETIZING TO PREDATORS, *CUTS A PIECE OF SPONGE THAT FITS PERFECTLY OVER ITS BACK*

THE STICKLEBACK
a fish WHICH BUILDS ITS NEST AT THE BOTTOM OF A RIVER, FRIGHTENS OFF PREDATORS *BY STANDING ON ITS HEAD*

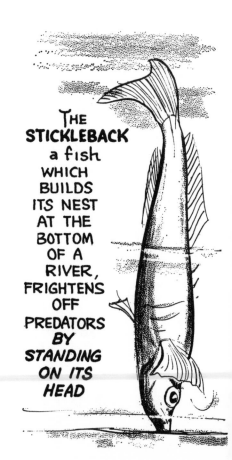

THE GLASS PERCH
of India HAS A BODY THAT IS *COMPLETELY TRANSPARENT*

½

THE **JAPANESE QUAIL** IS VALUED FOR ITS SONG, ITS EGGS, AS A FIGHTING COCK AND FOR ITS EATING QUALITIES — AND IN SOUTH CHINA IT IS CARRIED IN COLD WEATHER AS A HAND WARMER

THE **AFRICAN CATFISH** TO FIND ITS FOOD LEAVES THE WATER EACH NIGHT AND *CRAWLS ON LAND*

THE FEMALE WATER SPIDER LIVES IN A HOLLOW, BELL-SHAPED UNDER-WATER NEST WHICH SHE STOCKS WITH AIR BY BRINGING IT DOWN *IN BIG BUBBLES FROM THE SURFACE*

AN **EMPEROR PENGUIN** SHIELDS ITS YOUNG FROM THE COLD BY HOBBLING ALONG WITH THE CHICK *BETWEEN ITS FEET*

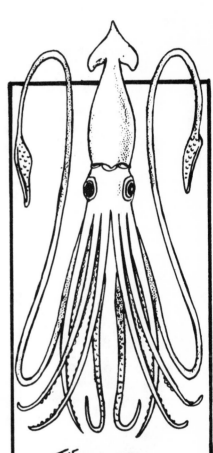

THE **SQUID** HAS THE LARGEST EYE IN NATURE — UP TO 16 INCHES IN DIAMETER

3 **PIKE** WERE HOOKED SIMULTANEOUSLY ON THE AVON RIVER, ENGLAND, IN 1925 *THE FIRST FISH HOOKED HAVING BEEN SWALLOWED BY A SECOND — WHICH WAS IN TURN GULPED DOWN BY A THIRD*

ROBERT LOUIS STEVENSON
(1850-1894)
FOUND THE PLOT FOR "DR. JEKYLL AND MR. HYDE" IN A NIGHTMARE

A. Lincoln

LINCOLN
☆

WAS BORN ON A
SUNDAY
FIRST ELECTED TO OFFICE ON A
MONDAY
TWICE ELECTED PRESIDENT ON A
TUESDAY
ADMITTED TO THE BAR ON A
WEDNESDAY
DELIVERED GETTYSBURG ADDRESS ON A
THURSDAY
WAS SHOT ON A
FRIDAY
AND DIED ON A
SATURDAY

THE **SATIN BOWER BIRD** of Australia
IN ADDITION TO ITS NEST BUILDS A WOOING BOWER TO DAZZLE ITS MATE, *LINING IT WITH RED BERRIES, FLOWERS, BITS OF COLORED CLOTH AND SHELLS*

THE **JINXED BUILDING!** FORD'S THEATER IN WASH., D.C, IN WHICH PRES. LINCOLN WAS SHOT IN 1865, WAS CONVERTED INTO AN OFFICE BUILDING WHICH COLLAPSED 28 YEARS LATER, **BURYING HUNDREDS OF CLERKS BENEATH TONS OF DEBRIS**

THE PIED-BILL GREBE
(*Podilymbus podiceps*)
BUILDS HER NEST IN THE FORM OF A RAFT--*ATTACHED TO REEDS SO IT WILL NOT FLOAT AWAY*

BENJAMIN FRANKLIN

THE STATESMAN, SCIENTIST AND INVENTOR,

WAS BORN ON JANUARY **17**, 1706, WAS ONE OF **17** CHILDREN, STARTED HIS CAREER IN PHILADELPHIA, PA., AT **17** AND DIED ON APRIL **17**, 1790

Submitted by RICHARD HEPBURN, MALDEN, MASS.

GEORGE SAND (1804-1876)

THE CELEBRATED NOVELIST WHOSE REAL NAME WAS AMANDINE AURORE LUCIE DUDEVANT, NEVER WROTE IN THE DAYTIME -- *DOING ALL HER WORK BETWEEN THE HOURS OF 10 PM AND 5 AM*

THE BOUQUET BUSH
Oleander
PRODUCING BLOOMS IN **20** DIFFERENT COLORS

Grown by NICHOLAS SIDERAKIS, Whittier, Calif.

THARP'S CABIN, THE HOME OF HALE THARP, DISCOVERER OF WHAT IS NOW SEQUOIA NAT'L PARK, IS MAINTAINED AS HE BUILT IT-- INSIDE *THE TRUNK OF ONE OF THE GIANT TREES*

THE 2-WAY ENGINE A LOCOMOTIVE BUILT FOR A 3-FOOT GAUGE RAILROAD In Venezuela, SO IT WOULD NOT HAVE TO TURN AROUND, *HAD 2 BOILERS, 2 CABS AND A COWCATCHER ON EACH END*

THE GENERAL WHO SAVED HIS LIFE BY BUYING THE WRONG-SIZED HAT!

GENERAL HENRY HETH (1825-1888) LEADING A CONFEDERATE DIVISION IN THE BATTLE OF GETTYSBURG, WAS HIT IN THE HEAD BY A UNION BULLET *BUT HIS LIFE WAS SAVED BECAUSE HE WAS WEARING A HAT 2 SIZES TOO LARGE - WITH NEWSPAPER FOLDED INSIDE THE SWEATBAND* THE PAPER DEFLECTED THE BULLET AND THE GENERAL, UNCONSCIOUS FOR 30 HOURS, RECOVERED AND LIVED ANOTHER 25 YEARS

THE TRAIN THAT GOES TO SEA

A RAILROAD TRACK LINKING THE GERMAN MAINLAND TO THE ISLAND OF SYLT, IN THE NORTH SEA, IS TRAVERSED FOR 7 MILES BY A TRAIN *THAT IS SPLASHED BY HIGH SEAS THROUGHOUT THE JOURNEY*

JOHN TYLER
(1790-1862)
10th PRESIDENT OF THE U.S., ENTERED THE COLLEGE OF WILLIAM AND MARY AT THE AGE OF **12**

THE **FIRST FLAG** OF THE CONFEDERACY WAS CHANGED AFTER ITS STARS AND BARS WERE MISTAKEN FOR THE UNION BANNER, AND FIRED UPON BY REBEL TROOPS

LANCE SKUTHORPE
famed Australian horseman
RODE 7 WILD HORSES IN A PERIOD OF 7 CONSECUTIVE MINUTES *WITHOUT EVER BEING THROWN*

ZEBRAS IN MEWAR, INDIA, ARE USED *TO PULL CARRIAGES*

FISH AND **REPTILES** CONTINUE TO GROW AS LONG AS THEY LIVE

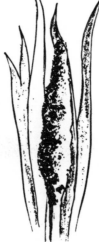

THE **CATTAIL** ON ITS SINGLE SPIKE *PRODUCES MORE THAN 1,000,000 SEEDS*

BABY SEA ELEPHANTS on the Prince Edward Islands, South Africa, CAN ONLY DIGEST THEIR FOOD WHEN THEY ARE *SUBMERGED IN WATER*

UNFAIR TO DENTISTS

THE **CROCODILE** NO MATTER HOW MANY TEETH IT LOSES *CONTINUES TO GROW REPLACEMENTS AS LONG AS IT LIVES*

THE **BOWHEAD WHALE** HAS A MOUTH ONE-THIRD AS LARGE AS ITS ENTIRE BODY

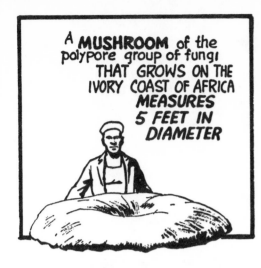

A **MUSHROOM** of the polypore group of fungi THAT GROWS ON THE IVORY COAST OF AFRICA *MEASURES 5 FEET IN DIAMETER*

THE BIRD THAT PLANTS A FLOWER GARDEN
THE GARDENER BOWER BIRD (Amblyornis inornatus) BUILDS A GARDEN ENHANCED BY COLORFUL BLOSSOMS AND SHELLS AND A SPECIAL HUT *AS A ROMANTIC SETTING IN WHICH TO COURT ITS MATE* THEY THEN SHARE A NORMAL TREETOP NEST

PEACE IS WRITTEN IN CHINESE BY A COMBINATION OF THE SYMBOLS MEANING "**WOMAN**" AND "**SUN**"

好

HEINZ ROX-SCHULZ A GERMAN WORLD TRAVELER, PAID FOR HIS TRIPS BY INFORMAL SHOWS IN WHICH HE PERFORMED HANDSTANDS *ON 2 BOTTLES PLACED ON HIS SUITCASE*

17 BROTHERS
THE SONS OF SIR DAVID MURRAY of Tullibardine, ALL SLEPT IN BLAIR CASTLE, Atholl, Scotland, *IN ONE HUGE CIRCULAR BED*

Ripley's Believe It or Not!

A CUSTARD PIE-THROWING CONTEST
IS HELD ANNUALLY IN COXHEATH, ENGLAND,
WITH COMPETITORS REQUIRED TO THROW A PIE
AT A TARGET FACE 8 FT., 3 ⅞ IN. DISTANT

A **PET POODLE**
WAS TRAINED BY LORD ERSKINE,
England's highest judicial officer,
TO SIT FOR HOURS WITH ITS
PAWS UPON AN OPEN LAW BOOK
WEARING A JURIST'S WIG

THE **LEAD** IN
THE AVERAGE
PENCIL WILL
WRITE
45,000
WORDS OR
DRAW A LINE
35 MILES LONG

ICE CREAM FRUIT
THE CHIRIMOYA, of Ecuador,
HAS A WHITE PULP THAT IS
SCOOPED OUT WITH A SPOON
AND COMBINES 3 DELICIOUS
FLAVORS – PINEAPPLE, BANANA
AND STRAWBERRY

HORSES
WERE SOLD IN
AUSTRALIA
IN 1924 FOR
1¢ EACH

**A NEW
ELECTRONIC
GAUGE**
USED IN MANUFACTURING
AIRPLANE INSTRUMENTS
*CAN MEASURE THE DEPTH
OF A MOUSE'S FOOTPRINTS
ON A STRAND OF WIRE*

THE FIRST WATCHES WERE
SO HEAVY THAT THEIR
OWNERS EMPLOYED
PAGES TO CARRY THEM!

JACK CARSTENS
of Kleinzee,
Namaqualand, S. Africa,
AND A FRIEND WERE
FISHING TOGETHER
WHEN THEIR HOOKS
SIMULTANEOUSLY CAUGHT
THE SAME FISH
*THEY CUT THE FISH IN HALF
AND EACH TOOK AN EQUAL SHARE*

IPOKRITOS
FROM WHICH THE ENGLISH "HYPOCRITE" IS DERIVED, ORIGINALLY WAS THE WORD FOR AN ACTOR OF ANCIENT GREECE

DR. I.H. ALEXANDER OF PITTSBURGH, PA., FISHING IN LAKE TIMAGAMI, CANADA, WAS SUDDENLY STARTLED BY A BEAR *THAT CLIMBED INTO HIS ROWBOAT*

DR. ALEXANDER COULDN'T SWIM, SO HE ROWED THE BOAT -- AND BEAR -- TO SHORE

$$1 \times 9 + 2 = 11$$
$$12 \times 9 + 3 = 111$$
$$123 \times 9 + 4 = 1111$$
$$1234 \times 9 + 5 = 11111$$
$$12345 \times 9 + 6 = 111111$$
$$123456 \times 9 + 7 = 1111111$$
$$1234567 \times 9 + 8 = 11111111$$
$$12345678 \times 9 + 9 = 111111111$$

MAGIC NUMBERS

$$473 \times 8 = 3784 \qquad 41 \times 35 = 1435$$
$$87 \times 21 = 1827 \qquad 351 \times 9 = 3159$$
$$93 \times 15 = 1395 \qquad 81 \times 27 = 2187$$

EACH ANSWER REPEATS THE DIGITS OF THE ORIGINAL NUMBERS

A BEAVER CAN FELL A TREE 5 INCHES IN DIAMETER IN 3 MINUTES

OPTICAL ILLUSION FIND THE **3 FACES** Drawn by ANTONIO D'ORAZI Eagle Rock, Calif.

THE **SHOES** WORN BY AUSTRALIAN ABORIGINES, HAVE SOLES MADE OF WHITE EMU FEATHERS *WHICH LEAVE NO TRACKS INDICATING DIRECTION*

TIMBER!

"MICHAEL" an Irish terrier, PLAYED IN 1,250 PERFORMANCES OF "PEG O' MY HEART," AND HAS BEEN CALLED A "CANINE IMMORTAL OF THE THEATRE" —YET HE WAS OBTAINED FROM THE LOS ANGELES POUND FOR $1 ONE DAY BEFORE HE WAS TO HAVE BEEN PUT TO DEATH

109

THE KIDNAPING THAT WAS FOILED BY A STORM!

RENEE NIVERNAS of Marseilles, France, A BABY GIRL 18 MONTHS OF AGE, WAS KIDNAPED FROM HER HOME ON AUGUST 4, 1908, AND HELD FOR RANSOM ABOARD A YACHT

A STORM SANK THE CRAFT AND ALL 8 KIDNAPERS PERISHED - YET THE LITTLE GIRL, SLEEPING IN A MAKESHIFT CRADLE OF PACKING CASES, FLOATED ASHORE AT CASSIS, FRANCE - *UNHARMED!*

THE **ELGIN BOTANICAL GARDEN** IN NEW YORK CITY, BOUGHT BY DR. DAVID HOSACK IN 1801 FOR $5,000, IS NOW THE SITE OF *ROCKEFELLER CENTER*

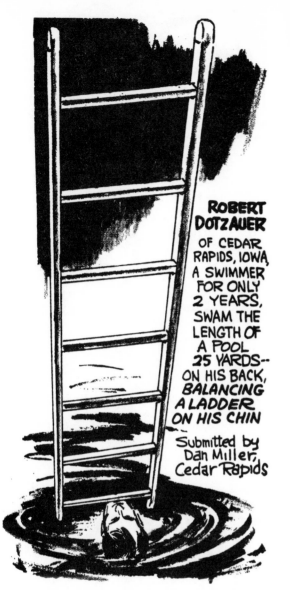

ROBERT DOTZAUER OF CEDAR RAPIDS, IOWA, A SWIMMER FOR ONLY 2 YEARS, SWAM THE LENGTH OF A POOL 25 YARDS-- ON HIS BACK, *BALANCING A LADDER ON HIS CHIN*

Submitted by Dan Miller, Cedar Rapids

LAMU

AN ISLAND OFF THE COAST OF EAST AFRICA HAS A POPULATION OF 31,000 YET NO WHEELED TRAFFIC IS PERMITTED ON THE ISLAND -*NOT EVEN A BICYCLE*

THE **"IMPULSORIA"** A LOCOMOTIVE INVENTED BY CLEMENTE MASERANO, AN ENGINEER FROM PISTOIA, ITALY, AND SUCCESSFULLY TESTED ON ENGLAND'S SOUTHWESTERN RAILWAY IN 1845 *WAS POWERED BY 2 TEAMS OF HORSES GALLOPING ON A TREADMILL*

Ripley's Believe It or Not!

AMERICAN CUCKOOS
DO NOT CUCKOO—
EUROPEAN CUCKOOS MAKE THAT SOUND,
BUT THE AMERICAN VARIETY ONLY CLUCKS

THE **MUSKOX**
FIGHTING A WOLF, LEAPS HIGH INTO THE AIR TO LAND ON THE WOLF ON ITS BACK

THE **RHINOCEROS** IS THE ONLY MAMMAL THAT DOES NOT HAVE TO BLINK TO LUBRICATE ITS EYES—FROM TIME TO TIME IT PULLS ITS EYES BACK INTO THEIR SOCKETS—AND TWIRLS THEM AROUND

NATURAL BRIDGE OF VIRGINIA

200 FT. HIGH — **90** FT. WIDE

GEORGE WASHINGTON SURVEYED IT AND CARVED HIS INITIALS ON IT. THOMAS JEFFERSON BOUGHT IT FROM *KING GEORGE III* FOR $5.00 !

THE **6-HORSE SLEIGH** used by the mother of Czar Peter the Great, of Russia, WAS ALWAYS ACCOMPANIED BY 12 GROOMS—ONE FOR EACH HORSE—AND 6 OTHERS WHO PUSHED THE SLEIGH TO INCREASE ITS SPEED—ALL THE GROOMS HAD TO RUN STEADILY FOR MILES

THE **GARDENER ANT** of the Amazon BUILDS NESTS OF MUD IN THE SHAPE OF A BALL AND TO HOLD IT TOGETHER PLANTS SEEDS *-WHICH MAKE IT LOOK LIKE A MINIATURE* **FLOWER GARDEN**

GOATS ARE TRAINED BY PALESTINIAN ARAB ENTERTAINERS *TO STAND ON 7 SMALL SECTIONS OF BAMBOO BALANCED ONE ON TOP OF ANOTHER*

BIRD'S-EYE VIEW HOMING PIGEONS EQUIPPED WITH TINY ALUMINUM CAMERAS WERE USED BY BOTH SIDES DURING WORLD WAR II *TO PHOTOGRAPH AREAS TOO HEAVILY FORTIFIED TO BE FLOWN OVER BY PLANES* THE CAMERAS WERE ACTIVATED BY AIR RUSHING THROUGH A RUBBER BALL

THE **GIRAFFE** HAS A TONGUE SO LONG IT USES IT TO CLEAN ITS EARS

"PROHASKA" AN AUSTRIAN WAR DOG **PARTICIPATED IN 20 BATTLES AND WAS WOUNDED 3 TIMES** AFTER ITS DEATH IT WAS GIVEN THE PERMANENT GRADE OF SERGEANT

ALLIGATORS DROWN IF HELD UNDER WATER

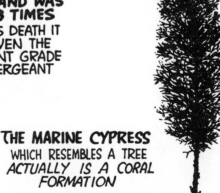

THE MARINE CYPRESS WHICH RESEMBLES A TREE *ACTUALLY IS A CORAL FORMATION*

Ripley's Believe It or Not!

THE MOST DARING ESCAPE IN HISTORY!
Nürnberg. Germany
—
EPPELEIN von GAILINGEN
—GRANTED PERMISSION TO MOUNT HIS FAVORITE CHARGER
AS HIS LAST REQUEST BEFORE BEING HANGED —
SPURRED THROUGH AN ENTIRE REGIMENT OF CAVALRY,
RODE UP A RAMP TO THE TOP OF THE CITY WALL,
THEN LEAPED HIS HORSE TO A MOAT 100 FEET BELOW
—AND ESCAPED WITHOUT INJURY
EITHER TO HIMSELF OR HIS HORSE!

A **BRIDGE** OVER THE KERAKA RIVER, in Nigeria, CONSISTS OF 3 TREE TRUNKS —2 OF WHICH ARE STILL *ROOTED ON THE SHORES*

THE **STINGING TREES** of AUSTRALIA HAVE LEAVES WITH HAIRS WHICH INFLICT ANYONE BRUSHING AGAINST THEM *WITH THE STINGING PAIN OF AN INJECTION OF FORMIC ACID—* THE SENSATION LASTS FOR WEEKS AND THE BEST ANTIDOTE IS APPLYING TO THE WOUND A SLICE OF THE STEM OF THE SAME LEAF

THE **SEAMAN** WHO WAS SAVED BY AN ALBATROSS

JOHN OAKLEY, HAVING FALLEN OVERBOARD FROM THE LINER "SOUTHERN CROSS" WAS NOT MISSED UNTIL THE BIG SHIP *WAS 20 MILES AWAY*

OAKLEY WOULD NEVER HAVE BEEN FOUND EXCEPT FOR A GIANT ALBATROSS WHICH THE SHIP'S CREW OBSERVED MAKING REPEATED SWOOPS AT THE BOBBING SAILOR - 1956

BUDS OF THE FOUNTAIN TREE OF INDIA, WHEN SQUEEZED, EACH YIELD A *FULL CUP OF WATER*

ZULU MOTHERS WEAR THEIR HAIR IN SUCH A MANNER THAT THEIR CHILDREN -RIDING PIGGY-BACK- CAN CLING TO IT

MUSICIANS In Bolivia PLAY REED PIPES *TALLER THAN THEMSELVES*

COCONUT PALMS SERVED IN TAHITI FOR CENTURIES *AS SUN DIALS* THE NATIVES KNEW IT WAS NOON WHEN A TREE WAS CIRCLED BY ITS SHADOW

THE TIGERS THAT DRINK SALT WATER
Sundarbans, India

THEY QUENCH THEIR THIRST WITH SEAWATER FROM TIDAL RIVERS WITH NO APPARENT HARM

EGYPTIAN FARMERS DAILY CROSS the Nile *ASTRIDE A LOG* -WHICH THEY PADDLE WITH THEIR HANDS

THE *STRANGEST* FISHING NETS IN THE WORLD

NETS used by New Guinea fishermen *ACTUALLY ARE SPIDER WEBS*

THE WEBS, WOVEN BY SPIDERS ON BAMBOO FRAMES LEFT IN THE JUNGLE, SHED WATER AND CAN BE USED FOR YEARS

FISHING BOATS in Nazare, Portugal, BECAUSE THE TOWN HAS NO HARBOR ARE HAULED ONTO SHORE WITH THEIR CATCH **BY TEAMS OF OXEN**

A DOG REALLY WAS THIS MAN'S BEST FRIEND!
JOHN CRAIG (1512-1600) of Edinburgh, Scotland, PENNILESS AND FRIENDLESS IN VIENNA AND FLEEING A DEATH SENTENCE, WAS AIDED BY A STRAY DOG— *WHICH BROUGHT HIM A WALLET CONTAINING SUFFICIENT MONEY TO PAY FOR HIS TRIP HOME*

SETTLERS TO GET AROUND THE HOMESTEAD ACT OF 1862, WHICH PROVIDED THAT EACH CLAIM HAD TO HAVE A HOME MEASURING AT LEAST "12 X 12," OFTEN BUILT MINIATURE HOUSES *ONE FOOT HIGH AND ONE FOOT WIDE*

1	ح	3	ع	ى
1	2	3	4	5
ى	٧	9	٩	0
6	7	8	9	0

OUR "ARABIC" NUMERALS EVOLVED FROM ARAB NUMBERS CREATED IN THE 6th CENTURY

THE **EQUIBUS** INVENTED IN BOSTON, MASS., IN 1878 HAD DRIVER, PASSENGERS -AND HORSE- *ALL INSIDE THE CARRIAGE*

THE **FIRST MOTORCYCLE** WAS INVENTED BY GOTTLIEB DAIMLER IN CANNSTADT, GERMANY, IN 1885, ONLY 60 MILES FROM WHERE KARL BENZ CREATED HIS FIRST PETROL-POWERED TRICYCLE *YET THEY NEVER MET*

A **SINGLE AMERICAN OYSTER** LAYS 500,000,000 EGGS A YEAR--*YET ONLY ONE OF THEM WILL NORMALLY REACH MATURITY*

JOSHUA HALL AN ITINERANT PREACHER of Maine, ALWAYS CARRIED 2 CANOES WITH HIM AND CROSSED RIVERS BY LASHING THE CANOES TOGETHER - *PLACING HIS HORSE'S FRONT LEGS IN ONE CANOE AND ITS BACK LEGS IN THE OTHER*

A **LOCOMOTIVE** FOUND ON AN ABANDONED TRACK IN BRAZIL IN 1907 WAS RESTORED TO SERVICE ALTHOUGH IT HAD STOOD IN THE JUNGLE FOR 30 YEARS AND *A TREE WAS GROWING OUT OF ITS SMOKESTACK*

THE **ANCIENT ROMANS** WASHED THEIR LAUNDRY IN VATS BY STOMPING ON IT WITH THEIR BARE FEET

HESSIAN SOLDIERS IN THE AMERICAN REVOLUTION, TO MAKE THEM LOOK TALLER, *WORE HATS 18 INCHES HIGH*

119

THE FAMOUS VOYAGE THAT OWED ITS SUCCESS TO CHOPPED CABBAGE!

CAPTAIN COOK (1728-1779) WHEN HE SET SAIL AROUND THE WORLD WITH 2 SHIPS IN 1776, EXPECTED TO LOSE 60% OF HIS CREW TO SCURVY, BUT THE 4-YEAR EXPEDITION DID NOT LOSE A SINGLE MAN TO THAT SCOURGE BECAUSE **COOK PRESCRIBED A STEADY DIET OF SAUERKRAUT.**

THE ONLY DEATHS WERE THE CAPTAIN HIMSELF, WHO WAS KILLED BY NATIVES, AND THE SHIP'S SURGEON, WHO SUCCUMBED TO TUBERCULOSIS

A Monkey in France WAS TRAINED BY THIEVES **AS A HOUSEBREAKER** IT WAS FINALLY CAPTURED AS THE RESULT OF A FINGERPRINT IT LEFT ON A WINDOWSILL

THE POLYPTERUS
A FISH OF TROPICAL AFRICA, BREATHES EQUALLY WELL UNDERWATER **AND FROM THE AIR**

THE BRITTLE STARFISH WHEN FRIGHTENED *SNAPS OFF ALL ITS ARMS*

THE SICKLEBILL HAS A TONGUE SO MUCH SHORTER THAN ITS BILL, THAT TO EAT, IT MUST TOSS ITS FOOD HIGH IN THE AIR *SO IT WILL DROP INTO ITS MOUTH*

DONKEYS in Afghanistan ARE SO SHORT THEIR RIDERS REST THEM BY DROPPING THEIR FEET TO THE GROUND *AND WALKING IN STEP WITH THEIR MOUNT*

THE **SINGING SEAL**

MARJORY KENNEDY-FRASER (1857-1930) FOLK SINGER OF HEBRIDEAN SONGS SANG "THE SONG OF THE SEALS" TO A GROUP OF SEALS ON THE COAST OF THE HEBRIDES in the North Sea *AND ONE OF THE SEALS RESPONDED WITH SEVERAL NOTES OF THE SONG -IN A PERFECT CONTRALTO*

THE **SILKY** A FOWL WITH WHITE BUSHY FEATHERS *HAS JET BLACK SKIN*

THE **FIDDLE THAT WALKS** THE MALAYAN MANTIS HAS AN ELONGATED NECK AND A BODY SHAPED *LIKE A VIOLIN*

Ripley's Believe It or Not!

2 CLOUDS PHOTOGRAPHED over Marseilles, France *BOTH SHAPED LIKE INVERTED FLYING SAUCERS* Nov. 4, 1954

THE **SHARK** THAT STARVED WITH A MOUTHFUL OF FISH
A FLOATING BARREL LODGED IN THE SHARK'S THROAT— *WHEN THE SHARK WAS FOUND DEAD — THE BARREL WAS FULL OF FISH* Jamaica - 1884

JOHN JOHNSTONE a professional diver CHECKING A CABLE AT THE BOTTOM OF BASS STRAIT *WALKED FROM VICTORIA TO TASMANIA - A DISTANCE OF 27 MILES - ON THE FLOOR OF THE OCEAN* September, 1948

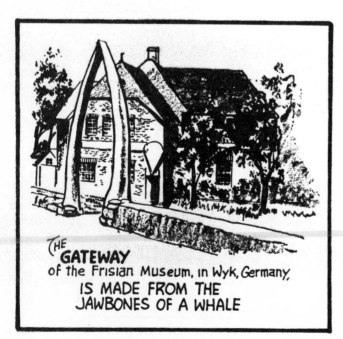

THE **GATEWAY** of the Frisian Museum, in Wyk, Germany, IS MADE FROM THE JAWBONES OF A WHALE

DOUBLE CANOES
OFTEN 150 FEET IN LENGTH, IN WHICH SOUTH SEA ISLANDERS MADE VOYAGES OF AS MUCH AS 1,600 MILES IN ANCIENT TIMES, ARE *STILL USED BY NATIVES* of Tahiti

THE **NESTS** BUILT BY **INSECT ARCHITECTS**

THE EUMENES DIMIDIATIPENNIS –a wasp– AFTER CONSTRUCTING 2 CELLS, *CREATES A "BLUEPRINT" FOR THE OTHER CELLS IN ITS NEST BY OUTLINING THEM WITH RIDGES OF MUD*

AN AURORA BOREALIS
SEEN OVER FINLAND IN 1932 WAS SHAPED LIKE *A CORKSCREW*

THE **DRUM** TREES OF **NEW HEBRIDES**
A GROUP OF TREES HOLLOWED OUT AND GROTESQUELY CARVED YET STILL SUPPORTED BY THEIR OWN ROOTS *SERVE AS THE DRUMS USED FOR INTER-ISLAND COMMUNICATION*

THE **CAVE WALLS**
IN RUINED CASTLES VALLEY, AUSTRALIA, ARE DECORATED WITH PAINTINGS OF HANDS, WHICH THE ABORIGINES CREATED *BY SPRAYING OVER THEIR OWN HANDS A MIXTURE OF WATER AND COLORED EARTH*

THE BROKEN-HEARTED OAK
AN OAK TREE CUT DOWN ON VALENTINE'S DAY LEFT A STUMP *SHAPED LIKE A HEART PIERCED BY A DAGGER*
Submitted by Andy Preslopsky, Dallas, Pa.

AMERICAN BUFFALO HUNTERS OFTEN STALKED THEIR PREY *WEARING THE PELTS OF WHITE WOLVES*
BISON HAD NO FEAR OF WOLVES AND ALLOWED THEM TO APPROACH

EAGLE HUNTERS
in the Hindu-Kush Mountains of Afghanistan
DISGUISE THEMSELVES BY WEARING THE *FEATHERS OF A LARGE HAWK*

SIOUX INDIAN PLAYING CARDS
MADE FROM THE SKIN OF DRIED FISH

THE WAR BONNET
OF AN INDIAN CHIEF CONTAINED AN ADDITIONAL FEATHER *FOR EACH GREAT DEED OF VALOR ITS WEARER HAD PERFORMED*

THE SHADOW BIRDS
ALWAYS BUILD A *3-ROOM NEST*
ONE SECTION IS A NURSERY, THE SECOND IS A PANTRY, AND IN THE THIRD THE MALE PARENT STANDS GUARD AGAINST INTRUDERS

CROSS SECTION

WASHINGTON WAS THE FIRST AMERICAN MILLIONAIRE

BOSS

"I CANNOT TELL A LIE" the "Boss" Lunch Milk Biscuit is the best in America

ADVERTISEMENTS IN THE LATE 19th CENTURY, OFTEN USED UNWITTING *ENDORSEMENTS OF THEIR PRODUCTS BY U.S. PRESIDENTS*

FERDINAND DURANG AN ACTOR FROM IOWA AND A SOLDIER IN THE WAR OF 1812, WAS THE FIRST PERSON *TO SING THE STAR-SPANGLED BANNER*

DURANG SANG IT IN THE PRESENCE OF FRANCIS SCOTT KEY AT BALTIMORE'S HOLIDAY THEATER IN SEPT. 1814, *2 DAYS AFTER KEY WROTE THE LYRICS*

125

THE WEDDINGS OF THE LOVE BIRDS

KHANDERAV –Ruler of Baroda, India,
INVITED. ALL THE NOTABLES IN HIS KINGDOM TO **42** MARRIAGE CEREMONIES
– THE BRIDE AND GROOM IN EACH CASE BEING
A PAIR OF PIGEONS !

KHANDERAV SPENT $2,000,000 IN THIS EFFORT TO CURRY FAVOR WITH THE GODS

THE STRANGEST STEAMBOAT—
THE WESTERN ENGINEER, FIRST STEAMBOAT TO ASCEND THE MISSOURI RIVER, WAS BUILT IN 1819 IN THE SHAPE OF A DRAGON TO FRIGHTEN OFF INDIANS —WITH ITS BOW A HEAD THAT SPEWED SMOKE FROM ITS MOUTH AND ITS STERN A TAIL THAT ISSUED A STREAM OF FOAMING WATER

THE **PUFFIN** DURING EACH COURTING SEASON, GROWS AN ATTRACTIVE EXTRA BEAK CONSISTING OF 9 SEPARATE MULTI-COLORED PLATES WHICH DROP OFF AFTER A FEW WEEKS

MA IN VIETNAMESE MEANS *BUT, YOUNG, RICE, HORSE, GHOST, TOMB OR MOTHER* --DEPENDING ON THE INTONATION

THE **PORTUGUESE FLY CATCHER PLANT** IS HUNG IN PORTUGUESE HOMES AS A LIVING FLY CATCHER

A **CHECK** FOR $15 WRITTEN ON THE SHELL OF AN EGG WAS CASHED BY A BANK IN VICTORIA, B.C.

"MR. McGREGOR" A SCOTTISH TERRIER OWNED BY JOSEPH DUDDY, OF PITTSBURGH, PA., REGULARLY RECEIVED EACH DECEMBER 25th AS MANY AS 300 CHRISTMAS CARDS

Ripley's Believe It or Not!

CHARLES GREEN
of London, England,
MADE AN HOUR-LONG FLIGHT
IN A BALLOON, SEATED ON
THE BACK OF A PONY
(July 29, 1828)

A **PUPPET**
CAVORTS FROM A ROPE IN
GERONA, SPAIN, EACH FESTIVE DAY,
COMMEMORATING THE HUMAN
ACROBAT WHO ENTERTAINED
THE POPULACE DURING A
DEVASTATING PLAGUE
500 YEARS AGO

CLASSROOMS in Luxembourg
ARE OFTEN
LOCATED IN THE OPEN AIR
IN THE DENSE FORESTS

THE
**FIRST
VIOLIN**
WAS CONSTRUCTED
BY PELEGRINO
MICHELI IN
MONTICHIARI,
Italy,
IN 1552
*AND IS
STILL IN
EXISTENCE*

ELEPHANTS
in Cambodia
SERVE AS BUSES BETWEEN
NEIGHBORING CITIES
*OFTEN CARRY AS MANY
AS A DOZEN PASSENGERS*

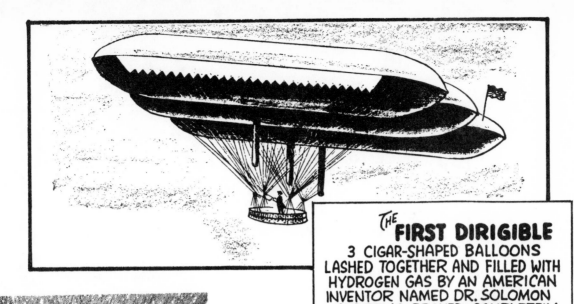

THE FIRST DIRIGIBLE

3 CIGAR-SHAPED BALLOONS LASHED TOGETHER AND FILLED WITH HYDROGEN GAS BY AN AMERICAN INVENTOR NAMED DR. SOLOMON ANDREWS PROVED COMPLETELY MANEUVERABLE AND COVERED 30 MILES IN 14½ MINUTES –IN 1863

THE GREATEST HORSEMEN IN THE WORLD!

THE *KAZAK KIRGHIS*
NOMADIC TRIBESMEN OF ASIA, WHILE RIDING THEIR HORSES AT FULL GALLOP
CAN PICK UP A CUPFULL OF MILK AND DRINK IT --WITHOUT SPILLING A DROP

THE MOST PRIZED SOUVENIR

SOUGHT BY VISITORS TO Cremona, Italy, HOMETOWN OF THE FAMED VIOLINMAKER, *IS A MINIATURE COPY OF A STRADIVARIUS*

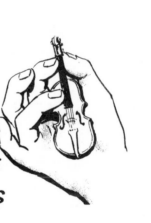

HO HUM

THE PARROT

IS THE ONLY BIRD THAT YAWNS

THE KIWI of New Zealand

HAS NEITHER WINGS NOR TAIL, IS BLIND IN THE DAYTIME, HAS ITS NOSTRILS AT THE TIP OF ITS BILL, AND *EACH DAY CONSUMES ITS WEIGHT IN WORMS*

A HUGE TORTOISE IN PORT LOUIS, ON THE ISLAND OF MAURITIUS, WALKED WITH 6 MEN ON ITS BACK
1850

THE SWIMMERS WHO WERE SAVED FROM DROWNING BY A WHALE

2 MAORI WOMEN, THE ONLY SURVIVORS WHEN A CANOE SANK IN COOK STRAIT, NEW ZEALAND, WERE SAVED WHEN THEY FOUND FLOATING IN THE WATER **THE CARCASS OF A WHALE**

A HARPOON WAS IMBEDDED IN THE WHALE, AND THE WOMEN PULLED THEMSELVES ABOARD THE CARCASS BY A LINE TRAILING FROM THE WEAPON --*AND FLOATED MORE THAN 80 MILES TO SAFETY* (1834)

MONKEYS ARE TRAINED TO **HARVEST COCONUTS** in Padang, Indonesia

THE NEST of the Agricultural Ant IS ALWAYS BUILT IN A DENSE GROWTH OF TALL GRASS—AFTER ENGINEER ANTS HAVE PREPARED A CLEARING AND BUILT A SYSTEM OF ROADS IN ALL DIRECTIONS

VITO DUMAS of Uruguay WHO CIRCLED THE EARTH ALONE IN A 31-FOOT BOAT, THOUGHT HE HAD RUN ONTO A ROCKY SHELF IN THE PACIFIC AT ONE TIME —BUT DISCOVERED HIS BOAT HAD BEEN LIFTED OUT OF THE WATER BY **2 HUGE WHALES** (1942)

FISHING RODS USED IN SPAIN AND PORTUGAL, HAVE AS MANY AS **10 HOOKS**

THE **LARVA** of the Sand runner CATCHES INSECTS BY DIGGING A TRAP IN THE SAND AND PLUGGING THE OPENING WITH ITS BODY. WHEN ITS PREY RUNS ACROSS THE OPENING THE LARVA MOVES AND THE INSECT DROPS INTO THE HOLE

THE **IRIDESCENT SEAWEED** (Iridophycus) WHEN LIGHT HITS IT, THE SEAWEED BECOMES SUCCESSIVELY **BLUE, GREEN AND PURPLE**

BEAVERS CAN STAY SUBMERGED FOR **11 MINUTES!**

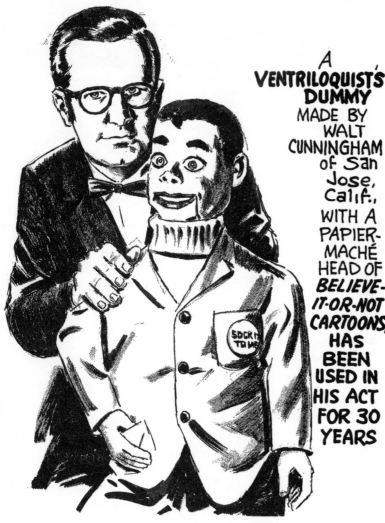

A **VENTRILOQUIST'S DUMMY** MADE BY WALT CUNNINGHAM of San Jose, Calif., WITH A PAPIER-MACHÉ HEAD OF *BELIEVE-IT-OR-NOT CARTOONS,* HAS BEEN USED IN HIS ACT FOR 30 YEARS

ROBERT GREER

A MATHEMATICS TEACHER AT THE MOUNT SCHOOL, in York, England, PROPOSED TO A GIRL NAMED ANNE IN 1880 WITH THIS MATHEMATICAL FORMULA:
IF $R=\frac{1}{2}$ AND $A=\frac{1}{2}$
THEN $R+A=1$
BUT R−A=NOTHING AT ALL
HER ANSWER
"LET IT BE R+A"

"BLACKIE" A DOG OWNED BY JOHN L. QUINALTY, OF MONTGOMERY, LA., SUMMONS HIS MASTER TO ANSWER THE TELEPHONE --*ALTHOUGH IT IS ON A 6-PARTY LINE* THE DOG ALWAYS RECOGNIZES QUINALTY'S RING AND IGNORES ANY OTHER CALL

THE **STIRRUPS** USED BY NATIVES of Marajo Island, in the Amazon River, Brazil, IN RIDING THEIR OXEN, ARE SO NARROW THEY *HOLD ONLY 2 TOES*

SALOMON VULPIUS
THE FIRST PUBLIC SCHOOL TEACHER IN STEGLITZ, A SUBURB OF BERLIN, GERMANY, WAS ALSO A TAILOR, AND FROM 1720 TO 1740 HE TAUGHT SCHOOL WHILE SITTING CROSS-LEGGED ON A TAILOR'S TABLE --*SIMULTANEOUSLY SEWING GARMENTS*

NATIVES of WhaKarewarewa, N.Z., COOK ALL THEIR FOOD IN FIBER BASKETS *LOWERED INTO HOT SPRINGS*

A **CHILDREN'S RAILWAY** IN HARBIN, MANCHURIA, COMPRISING AN ENGINE AND 4 COACHES, WHICH RUNS ON 7 MILES OF TRACK IN A PUBLIC PARK, IS OPERATED ENTIRELY BY CHILDREN UNDER 14 YEARS OF AGE

"**GOD BLESS YOU**" THE EXPRESSION USED WHEN SOMEONE SNEEZES ORIGINATED IN ROME IN 590 WHEN THE CITY WAS SWEPT BY A STRANGE PLAGUE MARKED BY FITS OF SNEEZING *POPE GREGORY DECREED THAT "DIO TI BENEDICA" (GOD BLESS YOU) SHOULD BE SAID TO ANYONE UNFORTUNATE ENOUGH TO BE SO AFFLICTED*

Ripley's Believe It or Not!

THE CHILD WHOSE COURAGE SAVED HER MOTHER'S LIFE
Nantes, France

ZOE de BONCHAMPS, ASKED TO SING BEFORE A FRENCH REVOLUTIONARY TRIBUNAL THAT HAD SENTENCED HER MOTHER TO DEATH AS THE WIFE OF A ROYALIST GENERAL, CHANTED: "LONG LIVE THE KING -DOWN WITH THE REVOLUTION!"

THE CHILD'S EFFRONTERY SO AMUSED THE JUDGES THAT HER MOTHER WAS GIVEN HER FREEDOM -AND SURVIVED FOR ANOTHER 52 YEARS. (1794)

THE LONE MERCHANT WHO DEFEATED A NATION IN WAR

JEAN ANGOT (1480-1551)
A SHIPBUILDER IN DIEPPE, FRANCE, INCENSED BECAUSE 2 OF HIS VESSELS HAD BEEN HARASSED BY THE PORTUGUESE, ATTACKED **LISBON WITH 17 SHIPS!**
HE CAPTURED THE HARBOR AND MANY VESSELS, RAVAGED THE LAND, AND BLOCKADED LISBON UNTIL THE **PORTUGUESE SUED FOR PEACE**

ADOLPHUS BEHRENDS

(1839-1900)
BECAME A SCHOOL-TEACHER IN NEW ORLEANS, LA.,
AT THE AGE OF 14

GEORGES SIMENON

WHO HAS BEEN CALLED THE GREATEST LIVING FRENCH NOVELIST HAS WRITTEN UNDER 17 DIFFERENT NOMS DE PLUME **MORE THAN 450 BOOKS**
HE ONCE WROTE A COMPLETE NOVEL IN **25 HOURS**

THE EXCLAMATION POINT

COMES FROM THE GREEK WORD "Io," MEANING: "I AM SURPRISED." THE "O" WAS FILLED IN AND PLACED UNDER THE "I" TO GIVE US: "!"

SCHOOL GIRLS
in Japan
OFTEN CARRY A YOUNGER
SISTER TO SCHOOL WITH THEM
ON THEIR BACKS

A **TOTEM POLE** in Old Kasaan,
on Prince of Wales Island
WAS SPLIT IN HALF
**BY A TREE THAT GREW
INSIDE THE POLE**
Submitted by Emery F. Tobin,
Ketchikan, Alaska

SMALL TREE-HOUSES
ARE BUILT
BY NATIVES
OF MUTHUVAN,
IN TRAVANCORE,
INDIA, **AS
PLACES OF
REFUGE FROM
ROGUE ELEPHANTS**

BABY EELS
TRAVEL IN
SUCH TIGHT
FORMATIONS
*THEY OFTEN
LOOK LIKE*
**A BALL
OF YARN**

THE **CATERPILLAR "CO-OP"**
AFRICAN PROCESSIONARY
CATERPILLARS
WEAVE A COCOON AS
BIG AS A FOOTBALL
*WHICH SERVES AS A
COMMUNITY HOME*
FOR 400 MOTHS

BOWS ARE MADE BY ESKIMOS OF THE BATHURST INLET, IN NORTHERN CANADA, *FROM THE HORNS OF A MUSK-OX*

A **ROCKING STONE** IN THE WALDVIERTEL DISTRICT OF AUSTRIA, SO DELICATELY BALANCED THAT IT CAN BE SET IN MOTION BY THE *TOUCH OF A CHILD*

BOYS OF the IRAKU TRIBE, Africa, TO SLIDE DOWN MOUNTAINSIDES *USE AS A SLED THE LEAF OF A LARGE CACTUS*

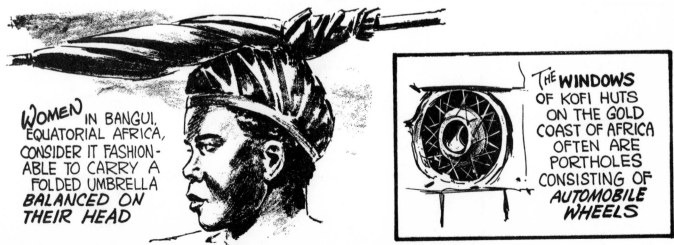

WOMEN IN BANGUI, EQUATORIAL AFRICA, CONSIDER IT FASHION-ABLE TO CARRY A FOLDED UMBRELLA *BALANCED ON THEIR HEAD*

THE **WINDOWS** OF KOFI HUTS ON THE GOLD COAST OF AFRICA OFTEN ARE PORTHOLES CONSISTING OF *AUTOMOBILE WHEELS*

Ripley's Believe It or Not!

THE **ICE-CREAM CONE** Phillip Island, Australia, *NATURAL STONE FORMATION*

THE **STRANGE SNOW FUNNELS OF THE HIMALAYAS**

HUGE CRATERS LINED WITH IRIDESCENT GREEN ICE HAVE SUCH A HYPNOTIC EFFECT

THAT TRAVELERS FEEL AN URGE TO LEAP INTO THE DAZZLING PIT

THE **"ADLER"** A GERMAN WARSHIP WRECKED BY A HURRICANE OFF Apia, Samoa, *STILL RESTS ON THE REEF ON WHICH IT WAS FLUNG* **78 YEARS AGO**

ONE-OARED SAMPANS OPERATED BY WOMEN ARE LICENSED IN HONG KONG HARBOR *AS WATER TAXIS*

MARCUS FIRMUS

A MERCHANT OF Seleucia, Syria, WHO PROCLAIMED HIMSELF EMPEROR OF EGYPT IN 271

OFTEN CONSUMED IN A SINGLE DAY A **300-POUND OSTRICH**

PORTABLE HOUSES USED BY NATIVES OF Northern Nigeria ARE MERELY LARGE MATS SEWN TOGETHER IN THE SHAPE OF A HUT —WHICH CAN BE SHIFTED EASILY FROM PLACE TO PLACE

WOMEN of Palimbai, New Guinea, FISH BY HOLDING BETWEEN THEM A HUGE NET WHILE *PRECARIOUSLY BALANCING THEMSELVES IN THE PROWS OF 2 SMALL CANOES*

THE TEMPLE THAT WAS SWALLOWED BY A TREE

THE PEROT TEMPLE on the Island of Java *HAS BEEN COMPLETELY ENMESHED BY THE ROOTS OF A GIANT FIG TREE*

THE "HAIRY FROGS" of the French Congo HAVE HIPS AND THIGHS COVERED WITH HAIR *AN INCH LONG*

RIPLEY's *Believe It or Not!*®

LOTTE FRUTIGER
CLIMBED MOUNT ALLALINHORN,
Switzerland
13,234 FEET HIGH AND ALWAYS
COVERED WITH ICE, IN 8 HOURS
- WHEN SHE WAS ONLY
8 YEARS OF AGE (Sept. 27, 1927)

DOORKNOCKERS in Morocco ARE MODELED FROM THE HANDS OF THE YOUNGEST GIRL IN THE HOUSEHOLD AS *A PROTECTION AGAINST EVIL*

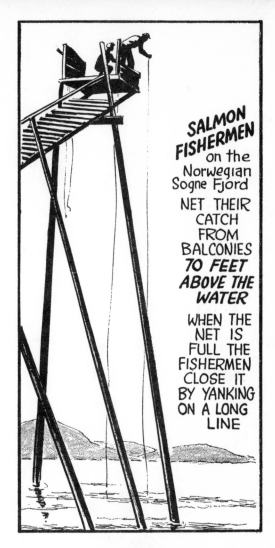

SALMON FISHERMEN on the Norwegian Sogne Fjord NET THEIR CATCH FROM BALCONIES *70 FEET ABOVE THE WATER* WHEN THE NET IS FULL THE FISHERMEN CLOSE IT BY YANKING ON A LONG LINE

ELIZABETH RANDLES (1800-1829) of Wrexham, Wales, PLAYED THE HARP AT CONCERTS BEFORE ROYALTY *BEFORE SHE WAS 2 YEARS OF AGE*

SCHOOLROOMS IN MANY VILLAGES IN NORTHERN CHILE HAVE NO TEACHERS, *SO THE LOCAL POLICEMEN INSTRUCT THE YOUNGSTERS*

RIPLEY's Believe It or Not!

BAYONA a little town in Spain, *WAS THE FIRST COMMUNITY IN EUROPE TO LEARN OF THE EXISTENCE OF THE NEW WORLD—* A SAILOR FROM BAYONA WHO MADE THE FIRST VOYAGE WITH COLUMBUS REVEALED THE SECRET TO FRIENDS

ERNEST G. BROGLIO OF THE SAN FRANCISCO GIANTS BASEBALL TEAM, PLAYING GOLF NEAR CHICAGO, ILLINOIS, HIT HIS FIRST TEE SHOT OF THE DAY-- *AND FOUND HE HAD DRIVEN THE TEE CLEAR THROUGH THE BALL*

EDWARD BRECHER OF BROOKLYN, N.Y., MADE A COMPLETE SET OF CHESS PIECES *FROM PEACH PITS*

MONTICELLO THE VIRGINIA HOME OF THOMAS JEFFERSON, HAS ONLY 2 EXTREMELY NARROW STAIR-WAYS BECAUSE *JEFFERSON CON-SIDERED THEM A WASTE OF SPACE*

ISABEL DE SOTO WIFE OF THE SPANISH EXPLORER *WAS THE FIRST WOMAN GOVERNOR IN THE NEW WORLD!* DE SOTO DESIGNATED HER TO ACT AS GOVERNOR OF CUBA FROM 1539 TO 1542 DURING HIS ABSENCE

LOUIS BRAILLE
THE FRENCHMAN WHO INVENTED A SYSTEM OF READING FOR THE BLIND, ADAPTED IT FROM MESSAGES USED BY FRENCH TROOPS WHO PUNCHED MARKS IN THICK PAPER SO THEY *COULD BE READ AT NIGHT BY FEEL WITHOUT USE OF A LIGHT*

A **HORN** CREATED IN THE AUSTRIAN TYROL, FROM *THE TRUNK AND BRANCHES OF A TREE*

SCOTT SUMERALL OF BROOKFIELD, MISSOURI, CAN PICK UP AND HOLD A REGULATION BASKETBALL *USING ONLY HIS THUMB AND MIDDLE FINGER* -- AT THE AGE OF 12

THE STRANGE STONES THAT COME AND GO
New Otago, New Zealand
THE MOERAKI BOULDERS, STONES AS LARGE AS 16 FEET IN DIAMETER, DISINTEGRATE AND VANISH FROM TIME TO TIME -- *BUT NEW ONES APPEAR IN THE SMOOTH SAND TO TAKE THEIR PLACE*

JOHN MERCER LANGSTON
(1829-1897), WHO WAS BORN A SLAVE, WAS ELECTED TOWN CLERK, IN LORAIN COUNTY, OHIO, IN 1855 -- *THE FIRST BLACK AMERICAN TO HOLD AN ELECTIVE OFFICE*

143

The **FIRST**
CIVILIZED AMERICAN!
B Franklin

INVENTOR of THE UNITED STATES

ALSO WAS THE LAST SON OF THE LAST SON OF THE LAST SON OF THE LAST SON OF THE LAST SON
HE WAS A SCIENTIST - PHILOSOPHER - MATHEMATICIAN - ECONOMIST - ADVERTISER - PROMOTER
- PROHIBITIONIST - ORGANIZER - HUMORIST - SATIRIST - EDITOR - MUSICIAN - ASTRONOMER - METEOROLOGIST
- POSTMASTER - FIREMAN - LEGISLATOR - DIPLOMAT - COLUMNIST - PROPAGANDIST - SALESMAN - PUBLISHER
- POLITICIAN - LOBBYIST - MORALIST - PUBLICIST - SOLDIER - ATHLETE - ARCHITECT - QUARTERMASTER - LIBRARIAN
- FREETHINKER

AND HE INVENTED
THE ROCKING CHAIR - HARMONICA - STREET LAMP - LIGHTNING CONDUCTOR -
DOUBLE SPECTACLES - FRANKLIN STOVE - CIRCULATING LIBRARY - MODERN
MILITIA - WHITE DUCK CLOTHING - DAYLIGHT SAVING TIME. HE DISCOVERED THE
IDENTITY OF LIGHTNING AND ELECTRICITY - THE GULF STREAM - BROOM CORN
THE FIRST SYSTEM OF VENTILATION - AURORA BOREALIS - VITAMINS IN THE SUNS RAYS
BALANCED DIET - MARSH GAS - BREATHING THRU THE SKIN - BENEFITS OF FRESH AIR
AND INVENTED THE SYSTEM AND TERM UNITED STATES OF AMERICA.